HOW TO BE SUCCESSFUL
BY BEING YOURSELF

'My search for meaning is over – thank you
for helping me return to myself'
Simon Jones, Global Reputation Advisor, Chime Communications

'The last success book you ever need to read'
Estelle Brachlianoff, CEO Veolia

'David is a truly inspirational writer'
René Carayol, CEO Inspired Leaders Network

'My nagging inner voice has gone – thank you, David'
Helen Gillan, General Manager NHS Blood and Transplant

'No one, that's no one, knows why people do
what they do, like David'
Adrian Gilpin, Chair, The Institute of Human Potential

'Yes, folks, he's back! And, boy, it's good!'
Craig Dearden-Phillips MBE, Founding CEO of Stepping Out

'Don't read this book unless you are prepared to have
the adventure your life has been waiting for'
Kathy Poole, People Director, Ascential

'It's like this book is written just for me –
and it will seem the same for you'
Alex Morley, CEO of Sanlam Wealth Planning

800 650 739

'It's time for you to come out from the shadows
and live the life that you were born to live'
Sally Hodgkins, Entrepreneur

'Change your life – and keep the change'
Tina Barnard, CEO Watford Community Housing Trust

'I wish I had written this book'
Claire Kidd, Entrepreneur

'This book simplifies how our minds work like no other –
it will drive psychologists crazy'
Bridget Dean, Project Manager

'How to be happy, without having to
actually do … eh … anything'
Marie Harrison, Strategic Programmes Director, Interserve

HOW TO BE SUCCESSFUL BY BEING YOURSELF

The Surprising Truth about Turning Fear
and Doubt into Confidence and Success

••••••

DAVID TAYLOR

First published in Great Britain in 2016 by John Murray Learning
An Hachette UK company.

This edition published 2017

Copyright © David Taylor 2016

The right of David Taylor to be identified as the Author of the Work has been asserted by
him in accordance with the Copyright, Designs and Patents Act 1988.

Database right Hodder & Stoughton (makers)

British Library Cataloguing in Publication Data: a catalogue record for
this title is available from the British Library.

1

The publisher has used its best endeavours to ensure that any website addresses referred
to in this book are correct and active at the time of going to press. However, the publisher
and the author have no responsibility for the websites and can make no guarantee that a
site will remain live or that the content will remain relevant, decent or appropriate.

The publisher has made every effort to mark as such all words which it believes to be
trademarks. The publisher should also like to make it clear that the presence of a word in
the book, whether marked or unmarked, in no way affects its legal status as a trademark.

Every reasonable effort has been made by the publisher to trace the copyright holders
of material in this book. Any errors or omissions should be notified in writing to the
publisher, who will endeavour to rectify the situation for any reprints and future editions.

Hardback ISBN: 9781473636316
Paperback ISBN: 9781473636323
eISBN: 9781473636330

Designed and set by Craig Burgess

Printed and bound in Great Britain by CPI Group (UK) Ltd, Croydon, CR0 4YY

John Murray Learning policy is to use papers that are natural, renewable and recyclable
products and made from wood grown in sustainable forests. The logging and manufacturing
processes are expected to conform to the environmental regulations of the country of origin.

Carmelite House
50 Victoria Embankment
London EC4Y 0DZ

www.hodder.co.uk

This one's for you
Because that is all you ever need to be
You
Just as you are.

To my daughter Olivia. The following conversation occurred when she was five, just as she was about to go to sleep:

ME: The biggest mystery of life is to discover who you truly are…
OLIVIA: Mummy, Daddy's scaring me again!

••••••

CONTENTS

TRUTH 1

......

IT'S ALL
ABOUT YOU

• • • • • •

Do you sometimes feel that your life is one endless roller coaster of busy-busy, and that there is much more you want to achieve in life, if only you could truly take some time out for yourself – to be calm, relaxed and re-energized?

Would you like to be in control of your life – how you feel, how you think and what you do, rather than having your feelings, thoughts and actions seemingly controlled by other people, by outside events and by your own unwanted negative thoughts?

Have you ever asked yourself the really big questions – 'Who am I, why am I here and what is the meaning of life?'

If you answered 'yes' to any of the above, this book is for you, whoever you are, however you are and whenever you are reading this. The three questions above are big, bold and brave. And here is a statement in the same vein that is the cornerstone to you achieving whatever you want – whatever you choose – in life: *no matter what your background, your education, your hopes, dreams and fears, everything you need, to achieve anything you want in your life, you already have within you.*

In short – there is nothing 'wrong' with you. And now we have got that out of the way, you can get on with answering

3

the questions above, achieving your biggest dreams, and helping others to do the same.

In your life, there will have been times when you were told that you were right or you were wrong; that you were good or that you were bad; or that you could, or couldn't, do something. These are, of course, simply opinions. The only indisputable fact about yourself is this: you are. You are you – just as you always have been. You were you on the day you were born – full of unlimited possibilities. And you are still you, now. And that is all you ever need to be.

Ultimately, we all want to achieve the same things: to fulfil the promise of our first few seconds, and to ensure that we have no regrets in our last. And no matter who you are, where you are or whatever you are thinking right now, happiness, success and spiritual fulfilment can be yours – indeed, they will be yours – when you know how to get them. Yes, we all need help at various points in our lives – but, most of the time, we simply need to know how to help ourselves.

......

'HAPPINESS, SUCCESS AND SPIRITUAL FULFILMENT CAN BE YOURS, WHEN YOU KNOW HOW TO GET THEM.'

......

This book will show you how by removing your inner voice of doubt, your fears and everything that is holding you back in life, and replacing them with more confidence, happiness and freedom. It will help you release the unlimited power, potential and possibilities that you already have locked deep within you.

It could well be that you doubt whether this is even possible. For example, perhaps when you read that phrase – 'everything you need to achieve anything you want in your life you already have within you' – you thought to yourself, OK, I want to walk on the moon without the aid of oxygen, or fly without wings, or teleport, and so on. And because these things are not possible – yet – you concluded that, if you can't achieve everything, you can't achieve anything. That is a frequent response to the words I have written, and the reason is that I believe we have a greater fear than the fear of failure.

••••••

'NO MATTER WHAT YOUR BACKGROUND,
YOUR EDUCATION, YOUR HOPES, DREAMS
AND FEARS, EVERYTHING YOU NEED,
TO ACHIEVE ANYTHING YOU WANT, YOU
ALREADY HAVE WITHIN YOU.'

••••••

Our bigger fear is 'success' – the idea that we can achieve so much more in our lives – dreams, outcomes and ambitions that are at present beyond our imagination. This is what really scares us – because such achievements and success are totally unfamiliar to us. And we don't like the unfamiliar. And so we carry on being uncomfortably comfortable – living the life we lead, while knowing we can each achieve so much more, and help others to do the same.

We fear success. And so we make up a massive lie about ourselves – that we have something missing. But we don't. Think right now about a fear that you have, and welcome that thought in as you read the words in the following tinted box.

> At the moment when you realize that you have nothing missing, that you find everything – you will no longer be lost, you will be *found*. And as you picture what that single word means for you, and knowing it is within your gift, your grasp, your choices, these thoughts are perhaps having a massive, positive, immediate effect on your energy, your wellness and your life. Right now.

I have promised what this book will deliver. What you have to do is really simple: read this book. And that's it – the results for you will be fast, lasting and extraordinary, and achieved with a minimum of effort, energy and struggle.

After all, your life was never meant to be a struggle. You won't have to spend all day reciting positive affirmations, or learning new and complicated terms from the world of mind, body and spirit books or do anything as drastic as moving into a monastery or nunnery. You don't have to stop living in order to rediscover how to live.

······

'YOU DON'T HAVE TO STOP LIVING IN ORDER TO REDISCOVER HOW TO LIVE.'

······

You will achieve a peace you may have been seeking for a very long time, or may have never before experienced. You will become relaxed simply by reading, and at last discover what this 'mindfulness' thing is really all about – not in theory but by experiencing it first hand. I will share with you the simplest, most effective and powerful techniques that work straight away, and continue working for ever.

Reading this book will quieten your inner voice of doubt, grow your confidence and give you a greater feeling of being in control of your time, your choices and your life – returning you to your birthright – living as a human being, not a human doing.

A human *being*. Life has conditioned us to be human doings. By that I mean we rush around, we're always short

7

of time, and life seems to get ever faster as we must do more and more and more. To remove these for good, while ensuring that you achieve more 'success' – by your own definition of that word – this book will:

- share proven, powerful and practical tips and techniques, which you can do straight away, and see the benefits of straight away.

- strip away the hype, jargon and mystery around why you do what you do, why you think what you think, and the psychology of you.

- be written for the way you are as a human being – not how you might think you are, not as others tell you that you are – but written for you, as you actually are.

Health warming (not 'warning')

To help you achieve these aims, throughout this book you will find tinted boxes with text that is particularly powerful for helping you be more confident, centred and calm – just by reading them. For maximum positive impact, please read these words more slowly, carefully and deliberately – saying them to yourself in silence as you read, in a voice that is calm, warm and kind – a voice you might use when speaking with a young child. Try it with the next example.

The more you are aware of these words and the spaces in between them, the more you may notice how your mind can begin to relax and space out a little. You may also notice that you are breathing in and out more slowly, deeply and naturally, and how with each breath you are perhaps choosing to be calmer, relaxed and more peaceful.

Welcome to a very personal and practical book written from an entirely new perspective – yours. Because your success is yours, and no one else's – yours to define, yours to own and yours to achieve – it will seem as if this book is written just for you. You will decide what success means for you and what you choose to do to achieve it. This book will seem to be just between you and me and no one else and as if I am writing, talking, engaging with you, and you with me.

Just as it does, right now.

The formula for success

The formula for success is significant, scientific and simple:

- **Significant:** this formula for success isn't new. It's just the same as every other success formula except with all the hype, jargon and mystery removed.

It's a formula that can be applied to anything and everything.

- **Scientific:** it is the very definition of what works, proved every day in the most rigorous way of all – does it work for you, according to criteria set by you, in the real world in which you live, every time?

- **Simple:** it is clear, concise and compelling. Simple, however, is rarely the same thing as easy. For example, while it is very simple to keep getting back up again after we are metaphorically knocked down in life, it is not easy to keep doing so. So it is simple, not simplistic.

The formula for success is also a way – a path, a journey, an adventure back to what you once knew, and have perhaps forgotten; back to when you had unlimited dreams and passions and your whole life in front of you, just as you do today; and back to remembering who you really were, and will be, once again. You will be reliving, reviving and remembering a very simple truth, one that has been buried over the years by all the 'should haves', 'could haves' and 'would haves'.

Whatever success means to you, it never happens by accident. It always follows an exact, proven and repeatable process. Every time you achieve your definition of success you will have followed this same process, from the moment you were born, to this very second, and every day forward, for the rest of your life.

This four-step process is shown in the following diagram and described in detail below.

The formula for success

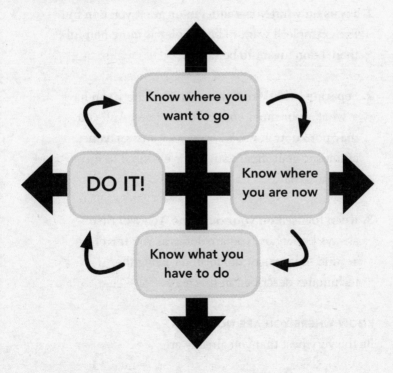

KNOW WHERE YOU WANT TO GO

You might call this your dream, your destiny, your ultimate goal or your outcome. Whatever you call it and whatever it is is for you and you alone to decide. Answering the following question may help you:

Imagine if you simply could not fail: what you would do?

To have the maximum chance of achieving your answer, take these steps:

1. **Focus on what you want**, not on what you don't. For example, 'I want to be happier' is more helpful than 'I don't want to be sad.'

2. **Separate 'what' from 'how'.** Immediately you have a 'what', your inner voice will ask 'how'. And you may not know 'how'. To keep your answer, your ambition, your dream alive, it is essential to focus only on 'what'.

3. **Keep focused on your outcome.** You will then always know how you are doing as you travel around the steps of the formula, using the techniques described in this book.

KNOW WHERE YOU ARE NOW

Be the very best that you already are.

Did you notice that, as you read those words, 'Be the very best that you already are', even though it may be an unusual phrase, you can perhaps picture, imagine, see yourself being just slightly more confident – it may happen as you read this, or take just a little longer.

To achieve your outcome, some people might tell you to be more than what you have become. Some people may inspire you to be the very best that you can be. I invite you to do something very different: simply decide to be the very best that you *already are*.

You were born with only two natural fears: a fear of falling and a fear of loud noises. You have overcome both – the first by learning to walk and the second when you were a teenager. That means that any fears, worries and even phobias that you have right now are those you have made up – you have literally constructed them in your mind. And with the right tools you can remove your fears any time you want, as you will see.

Please think about one such feeling you have right now that you don't want. Did you notice that just by reading this, word by word, that that feeling is starting to reduce, dissolve and disappear?

Being the very best that you already are means focusing on what you can do, not on what you can't. And what you can do is extraordinary, amazing and perhaps beyond your wildest imagination right now. But with the help of this book you will find that all things are possible.

······
'BE THE VERY BEST THAT YOU ALREADY ARE.'
······

KNOW WHAT YOU HAVE TO DO TO GET WHERE YOU WANT TO GO

You will never overcome your fears, worries and unhappiness with the same mindset that created them, just as you will never achieve your dreams, goals and happiness with the same mindset that stopped you taking action in the past. That mindset is one in which you will have been looking for answers outside yourself.

You need to stop searching outside yourself and start finding the answers within.

Removing your fears, and living the life that you were born to live, can happen only by transforming how you think, how you feel and how you live. That is why this book is written as it is – so that you can know, choose and transform your mindset to know that what you seek externally you already have, within you, right now. You'll achieve transformation by returning to be yourself – how cool is that?

......

'STOP SEARCHING OUTSIDE YOURSELF AND START FINDING THE ANSWERS WITHIN.'

......

DO IT!

Just by doing something – one thing – your brain, mind and memory will be redesigned – literally reprogrammed – so that you are more likely to do it again and again. Do it three times and it will become a habit.

And as you take each action set out in this book, please ask yourself: 'Is what I am doing now taking me closer to my outcome or further away?' If it is taking you closer, then do more of the same; if it is taking you further away, then do something else, and keep doing something different until you get closer to, and achieve, your outcome.

Or give up. Whichever you do, will be your choice. Choose to stop, or choose to get back up again and do something different.

Just as you have always known, deep down, as a child, that, if you did what you had always done, you would get what you always got. That is how you learned to walk, how you learned any new skill. And you are still as agile and adaptable, if you choose to be, no matter what your age.

How to read this book

Start at the beginning, continue until the end, and then stop. And, as you read, whatever you think, feel and believe is OK.

You have powers – strengths, talents and passions that are not separate from you. They are deep within you, waiting to be unlocked, and when they are it will literally astonish you. All you need to unlock them is the combination. It's as if your powers are in a safe – your own, private, personal, protected safe. No matter how complex you think the combination is, when you know it and use it, the safe will open.

It has to, it will and it does. This book is your combination – unique to you. And when it unlocks, you will no longer feel lost. You will be found.

The psychology of you

Experts are still studying, learning and debating how our brains work. The general consensus is that there is more we don't know about the brain than we do know.

For years, I have been obsessed about knowing what we do know, and then simplifying it down to a level that is understandable to a ten-year-old child, a Golden Retriever and me, who has the lowest intelligence level of those three. I then want to share it with the world so that people can apply this knowledge to help themselves and one another.

This book is written on the basis of what we know, which, when all the theory, jargon and mystery are stripped away, comes down to these three ideas:

- The brain exists to keep us alive – to enable us to survive – and it does this by making decisions very quickly, to conserve energy. The term 'gut feeling' could be more accurately renamed as 'brain feeling'.

- Because of this, the brain loves, craves and adores simplicity.

- The brain consists of two main parts – the conscious mind and the subconscious mind. There are other parts, with other names, that psychologists discuss, debate and disagree about.

It seems to me rather pointless that so much complexity, theory and different conclusions are written about something that thrives on simplicity – indeed, the brain probably cannot even understand what is being written about itself! This is why, here, I am going to radically simplify the brain – your brain, my brain, everyone's brain.

THE CONSCIOUS MIND AND THE SUBCONSCIOUS MIND
The following statement is made with all due respect to those highly qualified authors whose many books I have read, and whose long words I did not understand: we each have a conscious mind and a subconscious mind.

Your conscious mind is the mind in which you have your conscious thoughts – an average of about 20 a minute. Your conscious mind is your logical, sceptical protector – your nurture. You developed it from the moment you were born. This is often referred to as your ego, and that is the term I will use from now on.

Your subconscious mind has billions of thoughts – it is literally unlimited. It is your emotional, loving friend that you were born with it – your nature. Your subconscious mind runs your life subconsciously; you simply couldn't function if you had to be consciously aware of everything that you needed to do, think about and be aware of every day. This is often referred to as your self, and that is the term I will use from now on.

- **Ego = conscious mind = nurture** – that part of the brain or mind you develop from the moment you are born

- **Self = subconscious mind = nature** – that part of the brain or mind you were born with

Each of these has its own distinct voice:

Your ego voice is the one that chatters to you every day. In keeping you 'safe', it will often tell you what is 'wrong' with you, what you shouldn't be doing, and creating a general feeling of unhappiness. The ego voice is loud, unkind and judging.

Your self voice is a rarer voice altogether, drowned out by its ego counterpart. When it does speak, it whispers to you, telling you what is 'right' with you, what you could achieve and do, and creating a general feeling of happiness. The self voice is quiet, kind and loving.

For years, psychologists and academics have argued about which is more important – the conscious, ego level or subconscious, self level – and then came a discovery that rendered those arguments irrelevant. It was a discovery that took forward our understanding of the human mind, your mind, and how it works, by hundreds of years. And it is this: *whatever you believe at an ego level – in other words, whatever you believe to be true – your self mind makes it so.*

Do you believe that you have a great memory?

- If you answered 'yes', you will probably find that you remember things.

- If you answered 'no', you will probably find that you forget things.

- Either way, you will be 'right'.

'WHEN YOU BELIEVE
SOMETHING TO
BE TRUE, YOU SEE
THE WORLD
IN THAT WAY.'

Unfortunately for us, the same process happens when we think about something we don't want. In other words, whenever you don't want to think of something, you think of it. Right now, as you read this, do not think of a huge pink elephant, with a long tail, flapping side to side.

See? You can't help yourself.

Have you ever wondered why children almost immediately disobey you when you tell them, loud and clear, 'Don't touch the plates – they're hot'? It's because you told them to. It is impossible to not think about something, because to not think about it, you have to think about it...

The moral is: *be careful what you think about*. Focus on what you don't want and you will get more of what you don't want – it's a self-defeating spiral. However, focus on what you do want and you will get more of what you want – it's a self-fulfilling spiral.

So, in order to achieve the big changes we want to make in our lives, do we just have to believe that they are true with our ego mind? The answer to that is *sometimes* – there are tips, tools and techniques in this book that will help you do just that. Most of the time, though, in most of our lives, this is not enough. This is because the ego mind does not believe things lightly, for the sake of it. It needs convincing that what it is about to believe is true, proven and helpful.

Generally, people do not make radical changes in their lives because they decide to make these changes at an ego level. If this worked, everyone would be able to stop smoking, drinking, taking drugs or cheating on their diets and exercise regimes. In reality, a radical life change needs to happen at a self level.

The bottom line is that we are all driven primarily by our emotions – what we feel at any given moment in time. When it comes to logic versus emotion, emotion wins every time. This is demonstrated when we are upset or excited by a film (it's not real), scared of spiders (have you ever been mugged by one?), worrying about the past (totally illogical – you can't change it) or fearful of the future (it hasn't happened yet), and so on.

When it comes to what you are told and what you believe, your beliefs win every time. It is therefore only in the self mind that we can create massive, fast and lasting change. However, the most effective ways to access the self mind are through sleep (dreams), hypnosis and deep meditation, so it's no wonder life changes are not easy.

The result is that most people are comfortable being slightly uncomfortable. Deep down, people want to make change; they want to unlock their purpose in life. Maybe they want to discover their life's purpose, fulfil their inner passions or reveal their true personality. Perhaps they want to help others to break a habit or a phobia. But they never will, because they don't know how – until now...

......

'IT IS ONLY IN THE SELF MIND THAT WE CAN CREATE MASSIVE, FAST AND LASTING CHANGE.'

......

The solution

The Holy Grail of creating fast, massive and lasting change is to align the two minds – the ego and the self – as one, in harmony, in partnership. To put it another way, you need to speak directly to both parts – in the way they each prefer to be addressed. Then the ego will allow through what you are saying to the self – while also believing whatever it allows through to be true. Then, in turn, by believing it is true, the ego mind is supported by the self mind, and it not only becomes true but stays true.

And that is what this book does – every single practical workshop is worded in a way that aligns your ego and self, by convincing, in simple terms, the ego to trust what I am suggesting, so it hands over to your self to make the change, which then becomes permanent.

I discovered this technique during a bizarre experience in Northern Ireland. I am a qualified hypnotist, and a business leader asked me to hypnotize him to give him more confidence. When he arrived for the session, he was eating a sandwich, had clearly had a drink, and had only 30 minutes to spare. So I made the decision that I would simply have a conversation with him, using the same sorts of words, language and sentence structure that I would have done had he been hypnotized.

This was a shot in the dark for me, and it was very strange because, instead of having someone in front of me with their eyes closed, I had a wide-awake and stressed man eating a cheese sandwich!

But guess what? It worked.

It's fair to say that it didn't quite work to the same power as if he had been properly hypnotized. No, it worked better, a lot better. It worked better than if he had been hypnotized, because after hypnosis there is often an element of confusion in the mind of the person who has just been hypnotized. It clears soon after, but it is not a comfortable feeling.

As a result of that one incident, I decided to explore this further, and after much academic, personal and practical research I have come up with the technique that I call Predictive Persuasion – knowing how to ethically persuade yourself, and others, in a way that will work and that is helpful for the person being persuaded.

And that, of course, includes you.

This is the very powerful technique used in this book, which, as I have already said, is written in a way that will be absorbed by both your ego and your self. In other words, just by reading this book you will have a positive, relaxing and calming experience. You need to know that this is a totally manipulative book – it will manipulate you to find a peace that you may not have experienced for many years. However, I want to be fully transparent when I am manipulating you – hence the highlighted text in the boxes.

You might be thinking that your ego is now forewarned, armed and ready, looking out for that highlighted text. Yet this actually plays to the real strength of this technique – by indicating where the technique is being used, rather than hiding it subliminally, your ego, which is there to serve you in its own way, knows what is happening. Therefore it does not have to be on sentry alert. It goes quiet, gives its permission and simply lets the words, their sense and their impact through to your self.

Instant self-esteem

For now, right now, just pretend that your self-esteem is very high. Perhaps you could recall an experience when you felt extremely confident. How does it feel when you do that? When you think about what it feels like when you are self-confident, your whole body may suddenly feel the same confidence to some degree, without any effort at all: it feels very good.

This harmony between your ego and your self is very important, because both your ego mind and your self mind are there to serve you.

Your ego protects you from harm and fear and by saving you brain energy. However, it does its job all too well, and overprotects us. Real experts on the mind tell me that this goes back to the days when humans were prey to predators. And apparently that predator protection part of our brain is still alive and well and worrying us even to this day – it has been passed from generation to generation. This may be very useful for us if we happen to bump into a lion – in the shops, on the bus or just out and about – because we will know that what we have to do is run.

However, because this fear is not so useful in the modern world, this part of our brain no longer has a purpose. So what does it do? It finds a purpose. The ego's chosen purpose is to make us worry far more than we ever need to.

How to get your ego to pass thoughts to your self

There are three ways to persuade your ego to pass on thoughts to your self – through beliefs, boredom and bluffs.

BELIEFS

When your self already believes something to be true and the ego has the same thought, it will automatically seem to be true – in other words, when you believe something to be true, you see the world in that way.

For example, if you believe in, or don't believe in, a particular politician, it really doesn't matter what they say or what words they use; your beliefs will always be reinforced. If you have a fear of spiders, you will see one before someone who does not have that fear. If you buy a new car, you will suddenly notice other people driving the same model that you bought – especially if it's the same colour. If you decide to move house, you will suddenly spot all the 'For Sale' boards outside other houses.

BOREDOM

Your ego mind is more than happy to allow your self mind to get bored. That's why you tune out when someone is saying something obvious. You're being 'saved' from wasting valuable energy listening to something that doesn't need to be said. This explains why so many people daydream in work meetings and PowerPoint presentations.

BLUFFS

The ego mind switches off when it reads or hears or sees something that it doesn't understand, unless, of course, it's exciting.

> A person can, you know, let's call her Claire, understand
> things quickly and easily, especially when she thinks
> that you are in fact talking about Mike. As I mentioned
> to John, he told me that Michelle and Steve had had a
> long discussion with Eva, and she said, 'Just relax and
> go into a state of deep calm, now.'

Your ego gave up on my nonsense ramblings above, switched itself off, and that allowed me to give your self a simple, clear and immediate instruction.

Isn't this mind control? No – it is mind liberation. We have been controlled, persuaded and manipulated all our lives, and this book won't do the same.

Who manipulates us? A whole myriad of people:

- Our parents, who ensured we heard the word 'No' many more times than we heard the word 'Yes', thus making us masters at knowing what we cannot do (this was only because they loved us, by the way)

- Our schoolteachers, who more often taught us what to think instead of how to think

- Our friends, from whom we learned that 'success' needs peer approval.

Most of all, we are influenced by popular opinion outside ourselves – the way things are.

Take happiness. We would all like to be happy, or happier. And so we are encouraged to go out and look for happiness, to do things that 'make us happy'. Indeed, happiness is often seen as something we have to pursue, perhaps for all our lives. And all this does is push happiness further away.

Your happiness is not something separate from yourself – it lies deep with you. It was there on the day you were born, at every single moment, and is within you right now. Perhaps you can feel it – a warm relaxed and centred glow that you feel deep within you. So you can stop looking outside yourself for happiness. And if you choose, you can stop, right now. And in that very moment, you are happy.

And all these influences culminated in that internal, or infernal, voice that says, 'You are not enough.' This results in many people having a fear of being found out, of not being worthy of success, of feeling that they are some kind of imposter. Many people call this 'the Imposter Syndrome'. I call it 'the Imposter Phenomenon' because so many people have it. One of my main reasons for writing this book was to help people remove it. Not to cope with it, or fix it – because how can you fix yourself when there is nothing 'wrong' with you?

After many years, I discovered how to remove that ego voice that may be telling you that you are not enough. It will go quiet, dissolve and disappear. This is not mind control but the very opposite. This is mind choice, mind freedom and mind liberation. You will be more in control of your mind, rather than your mind being in control of you.

The only way to control your mind is to set it free. And that is what you are about to do. Mind control works only if you believe that you are not enough, that you have something missing, that you have a lot to learn and so on. Mind freedom is knowing that you *are* enough, just as you are.

It's the very same freedom you knew on the day you were born.

......

'THE ONLY WAY TO CONTROL YOUR MIND IS TO SET IT FREE.'

......

Time to reflect

You are wherever you are, right now, reading this.
Now that may not read as a particularly persuasive line, sentence, and nine words.

With that in mind, please reread it, and this time as you read, whoever you are, wherever you are and whenever you are reading this, it could be that you are feeling more calm, relaxed and at peace.

You are wherever you are, right now, reading this.
More calm, centred and confident – just by reading, you are breathing more deeply and perhaps your pulse has slowed. Or perhaps you are simply going with the flow. Whichever you choose is OK.

You are wherever you are, right now, reading this.
Please keep rereading that line, focusing your awareness this time on each word, on each letter within each word, and on the silent space between each word. Now you notice that your comfort and relaxation begin to deepen. You are breathing more slowly and your heart rate has slowed as you deepen your feeling of peace more and more completely, and enjoy the experience thoroughly.

Have you ever thought about you, and everyone around you, in that way? It is the sort of information that seems so impossible and yet so engaging that you may lose yourself in thinking about it. Have you ever wondered what it is like being so lucky, being born, being here? And have you noticed, right now, how you feel warm, relaxed and inspired?

TRUTH 2

• • • • • •

YOU WERE BORN
TO BE YOU

• • • • • •

You will have seen the big promise in bookshops and online many times: 'Lose yourself in a book.' Truth 2 makes you an even bigger promise: 'Don't lose yourself in a book; find yourself in one.' This one.

Do you believe in miracles?

Let's start by defining a miracle; you may prefer the term 'earthly miracle'. A miracle is a highly improbable or extraordinary event, development or accomplishment. This, at least, seems to be the most common definition.

What do you think constitutes 'highly improbable' or 'extraordinary'? One in a billion? Not enough? One in a trillion? Still not a 'miracle'? OK, let's jump a bit – how about 1 in 400 trillion (4×10^{14})? Even the most sceptical of you must think that any event with these odds would basically never happen. And yet there is one such event in real life that has these odds, odds that the scientist Richard Dawkins says are so great that this event has no chance of happening – no scientific chance whatsoever.

And that event is you.

Being a positive person, I often talk about death, and how important it is to ensure that you have no regrets in your final few moments on this earth. And then I read this:

······

'WE ARE GOING TO DIE, AND THAT MAKES US THE LUCKY ONES. MOST PEOPLE ARE NEVER GOING TO DIE BECAUSE THEY ARE NEVER GOING TO BE BORN. THE POTENTIAL PEOPLE WHO COULD HAVE BEEN HERE IN MY PLACE BUT WHO WILL IN FACT NEVER SEE THE LIGHT OF DAY OUTNUMBER THE SAND GRAINS OF ARABIA. CERTAINLY THOSE UNBORN GHOSTS INCLUDE GREATER POETS THAN KEATS, SCIENTISTS GREATER THAN NEWTON. WE KNOW THIS BECAUSE THE SET OF POSSIBLE PEOPLE ALLOWED BY OUR DNA SO MASSIVELY EXCEEDS THE SET OF ACTUAL PEOPLE. IN THE TEETH OF THESE STUPEFYING ODDS IT IS YOU AND I, IN OUR ORDINARINESS, THAT ARE HERE. WE PRIVILEGED FEW, WHO WON THE LOTTERY OF BIRTH AGAINST ALL ODDS.'

······

Richard Dawkins,
Unweaving the Rainbow: Science, Delusion and the Appetite for Wonder (Allen Lane, 1998)

From a scientific and statistical point of view, you should not exist. And yet you do – which makes you a miracle. Now do you believe in miracles (earthly ones)? In other words, do you believe in you?

Those of you who are sceptical will now be thinking, 'Those figures can't be right.' And the sceptics are right – although this is a statistic I have been quoting with great drama, excitement, it is completely, totally and factually wrong…so maybe you are not a miracle at all.

No, the actual chances of you being on this planet are so vast that the term 'miracle' doesn't begin to do them justice, because those odds of 400 trillion to 1 against don't take into account the chances of your mum meeting your dad, that they stay together long enough to have kids, that one particular egg happened to meet one particular sperm… We are now up to 1 in 400 quadrillion – 1 in 400,000,000,000,000,000. That is approximately the volume of water in cubic metres of the Atlantic Ocean.

Hang on, though – there is another factor at play here – namely that every one of your ancestors going back 4 billion years lived to an age where they could reproduce, and did reproduce…

Now we reach a staggering figure – 1 in 10 to the power of 2,685,000. ($1 \times 10^{2,685,000}$).

That's a 10 with 2,685,000 zeros after it.

Think of it like this: it is the probability of 2 million people getting together each to play a game with trillion-sided dice. They each roll the dice, and they all come up with the exact same number, for example 550,343,279,001. (*Source*: http://visual.ly/what-are-odds).

And yet, here you are… and on the day you were born, you were enough, just as you were. And today you are enough, just as you are.

> Is this amazing statistic enough for you to appreciate now, or will it take a little time for you to reflect and for it to sink in? And how would you live when you know you are such a miracle? Deep down, how would you be, breathe, and believe? How will your internal awareness, being, self, grow?

Now you know that you are a miracle, or unique, and understand the sheer unlikelihood of your being alive to read this – whatever words work for you – then please don't keep your strengths, your ideas and your passions a secret anymore. It is time for you to come out from the shadows and live the life that only you were meant to live. A life that can't be lost or won, but simply played, lived and loved. You were born – you got lucky – that's what started you. Now who is stopping you, and why must they fail?

••••••

'IT'S TIME TO COME OUT FROM THE SHADOWS AND LIVE THE LIFE YOU WERE MEANT TO LIVE.'

••••••

Truth 2: You were born to be you

All those who have told you, or will tell you, that there is indeed something wrong with you have a vested interest in doing so. This includes the thriving self-help industry (otherwise how could they sell any books?), the media (bad news travels), your parents (out of love and not wanting you to be disappointed in life), your teachers (to grade you), and your peers (for all sorts of reasons).

I am very fortunate to work with people from all walks of life. They include people who use wheelchairs, people who are sight-impaired, and people who have been diagnosed as 'depressed', with phobias and fears, or addicted to alcohol and drugs. And there is nothing 'wrong' with any of them, with any of us or, indeed, with you.

Of course, we all have things we cannot do, for all sorts of reasons. I just don't think it helps to focus on what we can't do. It is much more helpful, hopeful and rewarding to focus on what we can do. I do not believe that people should be defined by what is 'wrong' with them. Don't misunderstand me; we all have bad days, low points, times when we are fearful, scared and unhappy. This book is written for that very reason, to remove those unhelpful feelings – those that disempower and weaken you – and replace them with helpful ones – those that empower and strengthen you.

When you do this, and do this you will, it puts you in a place where you can more successfully deal with the issues, problems and challenges that we all face in life, and to take advantage of the opportunities, achievements and ambitions that are open to you in your life. In both of these you will be able to clear your mind and think clearly and correctly – in terms of seeing the best ways forward and actually doing something about it.

We are often told that, when we are faced with pressure, we have three 'natural' responses – fight, flight or freeze. This book gives you a fourth option – focus.

Just pretend for a moment that you could remember what it felt like to come into this world. When you make-believe and imagine what you felt like, you are having the same experience at the same level. You have a feeling of joy, warmth and of having fulfilled your self-quest – to be born. Never again, except perhaps now, will you know the true feeling of self – a spiritual, everlasting, loving friend. Can you perhaps experience these feelings as if you were a baby being rocked to sleep in your mother's arms?

Imagine if you were stripped of all the 'king's new clothes' that have together falsely convinced you that you are not enough – the anger, unhappiness or fear – the feelings, emotions and behaviours that you learned from others. Perhaps you are thinking it is time to strip away the imagined king's new clothes – the falsehoods that are holding you back – and realize that your future success as an individual, in your relationships and in your career, comes from within, not without.

Truth 2: You were born to be you

When you do that, all you have left is you, and that is all you ever need. And if that isn't the very definition of authentic, of honest, or of truth, I don't know what is. You are here, right now. Exactly as you are, and exactly as you once were and always will be. Just so.

Your life was never meant to be a struggle. It was meant to be a joy, a wonder and an adventure full of fun, choices and pleasures, just as you thought it was when you were young. Maybe you wanted to be a doctor, a teacher or a firefighter. You had powerful dreams and a powerful belief that you could make those dreams come true. And it is just the same today. You can have powerful dreams and have the powerful belief that you still can make them come true. Why should dreams be only for children? Why can't 'adults' dream as well?

What's it like when you remember a wonderful experience you had when you were young, thinking about what you wanted to 'be' when you grew up? When you think about it – see what you saw, hear what you heard, feel what you felt – you are young and excited again. Age is not a time thing; it is a choice thing. And you can recall these powerful, positive feelings subconsciously, without any effort at all.

From your very first day, when you were the most perfect, fragile and precious thing, you were ready, hungry, even ravenous, to take in as much knowledge and experience as you could. The pupils in your eyes would have felt as big as saucers, as you took it all in – everything going on around you.

You heard opinions as if they were facts, because they were expressed as being true. You listened to people's beliefs and took them as rules. You were fascinated, curious and wowed by a boiling kettle, only for your caring, loving, protective parents to say, in a loud voice: 'No no no no no no no no no no no no…'

As children, we heard the word 'no' many more times than we heard the word 'yes'. If you were a very active, lively and curious child, you may well have heard 'no' hundreds of times every day! And while the word kept us safe, it was also the perfect conditioning, learning and training for us to be masters – genius – at knowing what we cannot do.

The battle between ego and self

The battle – a sort of mental boxing match – between your ego mind and your self mind began the moment you were born:

- In the blue corner is your self that you were born with – your natural calmness, confidence and curiosity.

- In the red corner is your ego that you are being taught – your ego being formed by the opinions of others, stated as facts.

In the early battles, your self would be reinforced by ego – everyone looked at you with love, warmth and a smile. You even learned to walk, something that it is not possible to explain with words (go on, try to without moving your legs). Then, as you grew older, self will have started to conflict with ego. You learned that certain behaviours would be rewarded with cuddles and that other behaviours were 'naughty'.

Psychologically and scientifically, the concept of 'mine' is inbuilt in children. We have to learn the concept of empathy and sharing. Children are completely egocentric until the age of around three or four; they do not understand other people's feelings or thoughts and cannot place themselves in others' shoes until they are more developed. By this age, your protective ego was almost fully formed – you needed more sleep, more love, more food, more of your parents' time, more of everything.

······
'THE EGO IS NEVER SATISFIED – IT ALWAYS WANTS MORE.'
······

Your ego constantly tells you that you are not enough, and so you work harder, you keep going, and even when you achieve your 'success', you feel that you have to go further. The problem with your ego is that it can never be satisfied. It may get a moment's satisfaction at someone else's misfortune, it may even turn itself off at night, but sooner or later it is back telling you to go further, go faster, aim higher.

Your ego thinks it is helping us. It is ensuring that we comply with the conditioning we have learned throughout our lives, saying things like 'Keep your feet on the ground', 'Don't trust people who give you compliments', 'Life is hard so you must try harder, or you will be a failure.' In short, our ego keeps us 'safe' by its own definition, where 'safe' means 'familiar'. I do not believe in 'comfort zones' because most people said to be in 'comfort zones' are actually extremely uncomfortable. I think we have 'familiarity zones'. Our conditioning, our logical ego mind, our ego, will do anything to keep our lives familiar.

Our ego acts like our parents. Just as our parents may have pointed out the huge challenges to achieving our heady goals and ambitions because they did not want us to fail and be disappointed, the ego has learned to help us avoid disappointment like the plague, and so it will protect us from anything unfamiliar.

The chances are that, at some stage in your life, ego won, and that it still thrives on the word 'more' – more possessions, more superficiality (clothes, looks, etc.) and more money. And in return for getting more of everything, your ego promises you that, one day, you will be 'happy'.

The ego's ultimate trick is convincing you that many of the unhelpful beliefs that it taught you were entirely natural and factual. (For example, people may say 'I'm a born cynic' but this is a ridiculous statement – a cynic would not have even left the womb.) And so it looks as if ego wins… or does it? The wonderful, amazing and true answer is 'no'.

What would it be like if every word that has been read since you started reading this book, every sentence and every page, have brought you to this point? Just imagine, for a moment, that every thought, every moment and every choice you have ever made have brought you to this very moment. How powerful would that be? And it is exactly that – you are you. You are the unique, miraculous, wondrous you – reading this right now. Imagine that this is exactly where you ought to be in your life.

The good news, the great news, the most magnificent news, is that, while ego may have won, self didn't lose.

Self persuaded ego that you needed both of them to survive, and ego agreed, on condition that both parties understood that ego knows best. And so ego, newly established as your ego, said that it would allow new ideas or thoughts or experiences through to self only if it chose to – it took control. With little choice, your self went quiet, and waited.

Ego played its new role to perfection. It filtered out meanings, opinions and truths to suit itself. It allowed only those new experiences that wouldn't threaten you or its own status – getting on planes, going on a roller coaster, dreaming and so on. And a constant in all this was the ego's insistence that you are not enough; an idea fuelled by its own self-interest. After all, if you were actually enough, you wouldn't know what to do, would you? other than live… really *live*. Because here you are you; here you were, here you are and here you always will be – remembered long after you leave this planet in stories that will almost always be positive, funny and fond.

WORKSHOP:
Write your own eulogy

I want you to write your own eulogy as it would be read at your funeral. These words should reflect what you did in your life and what you achieved, and it should be all about you.

Write it now.

Done?

Now read it aloud, ideally to someone who knows you really well.

Is that how you are living your life right now? If the answer is 'yes', you can choose to change nothing. You can choose to go help a loved one or friend do the same thing.

If the answer is 'no', ask yourself, 'What am I going to do about it?'

If God – whatever those three letters mean to you – had wanted you to be 'naked', you would have been born that way. And so you were: naked, ready to fulfil the promise of your first few seconds. And perhaps as you think about that, whoever you are, you drift now into a calm, quiet, peaceful state of mind. This is your self – your true spiritual, everlasting, loving friend awakening once again. And deep down, deeper than your ego mind can ever know, make up or imagine, you have always known this. That you, being you, is not just magnificent, miraculous: it is also OK. You are OK, just as you are.

Getting through to your ego

To get through to your ego, many people recommend making positive affirmations like:

- 'I am confident.'
- 'I can do this.'
- 'I am gorgeous.'

The challenge with this approach is that these affirmations take a lot of repetition, because the ego will call them into question, as it does all truths that don't serve its need. If you repeat them often enough, they may work for you, and this book is all about what works for you – what always works for you – whoever you and wherever you are.

However, the simple technique I recommend is another way to get through to your ego. It's a faster, simpler, more powerful way that works for everyone. It will have an immediate, positive impact on you from the moment you read of it and do it.

It's simply this: *ask yourself helpful questions.*

ASK YOURSELF HELPFUL QUESTIONS

You may have personally experienced the negative power of unhelpful questions you have said to yourself, either out loud or in your mind. Either way it has the same unhelpful impact:

- Maybe you have bumped into the corner of the bed after just getting up and asked yourself, 'Why am I so clumsy?'

- Maybe you have forgotten something and asked yourself, 'Why is my memory so bad?'

- Maybe you have said the wrong thing at the wrong time and asked yourself, 'Why don't I think before I speak?'

We know how negatively powerful this is. Now let's use exactly the same principle in the positive. From now, you will experience the power of helpful questions you ask yourself, either out loud or in your mind – either way has the same helpful impact:

- You successfully navigate the corner of the bed after you have just got up and you ask yourself, 'Why am I so awake and alert first thing in the morning?'

- You remember something and you ask yourself, 'Why is my memory so perfect?'

- You say the right thing at the right time and you ask yourself, 'Why am I so good at thinking about what to say?'

······

'ASK YOURSELF HELPFUL QUESTIONS.'

······

This technique works for three reasons:

1. The questions automatically assume that what you are asking is true. There is no doubt about whether this is true or not for the ego to pick up on. Similarly, in those unhelpful questions, the ego agrees without challenge. Let's ask helpful questions where the ego agrees without challenge.

2. Every time you say, think or believe something negative or positive about yourself, and especially if someone else says the same to you, it rewires our brains and has a direct physical effect on the chemistry of our body. Recent science has proved that we can, in effect, choose our own psychological make-up.

3. Helpful questions are not threatening to anyone.

DO SOMETHING DIFFERENT

Another very powerful way to experience the power of questions is this: make a change in your life by doing something different, for instance by eating a piece of fruit instead of a chocolate bar. As you do so, ask yourself this:

'Can I remember, way, way back, long ago, when I made that decision to eat healthier food – wow, that seems like ages ago now – how many months was it?'

Just by doing this, you will recode your memory that it was ages ago, even if it was only a day ago!'

......

'MAKE A CHANGE IN YOUR LIFE BY DOING SOMETHING DIFFERENT.'

......

Why do questions hold such power over us and within us? What is it like when you think about that? Do you perhaps start to feel slightly stronger, more empowered, maybe even a little taller? The fact is that, as you are reading this, you are changing the very make-up of your body chemistry and that experience itself is simply amazing. Isn't is truly wondrous, how science has made all these amazing discoveries in your lifetime, so that you can truly decide, right now, to live the life you were born to lead?

Getting through to your self

I am now going to whisper something to you, and because of the build-up to this point, when you read, hear and take it in my words, on the following page, you will have a moment of perfect bliss, of total peace and a realization of an amazing truth that you have always known and will now know once again.

`IT'S OK
IT'S OK
IT'S ALWAYS OK.
EXCEPT WHEN IT'S NOT
AND THAT'S OK AS WELL.´

It's as if those words, 'It's OK', those five letters plus an apostrophe, are leaving the surface of the page and running through your body like beautifully warm water in a bath. Suppose those feelings are reaching the very centre of your being, right now. Can you imagine how wonderful that feeling must be right now?

WORKSHOP:
Choose your state of being

Now, as you truly live in this moment, and every word automatically follows the previous one, you can choose if you wish to feel calm, abundant and at total peace. Very good.

1. Now, take those feelings of now, of wow, and double them.

2. That's right.

3. Now double them again.

4. Now remember a time in your life when you felt this confident, certain and centred. Close your eyes for a few moments and see where you were in your mind, hear what you heard and feel what you felt. Take as long as you choose.

5. And, feeling as wonderful as you now do, discreetly touch the tip of the first finger of your left hand with your thumb. And feeling the gentle pressure between thumb and finger, please close your eyes once again.

6. Now separate your thumb and finger.

You now have two proven, practical and powerful ways to immediately change and choose your state of being, wherever you may be in life: 'It's OK', and the touching of your thumb and finger.

You have some very simple words: It's OK.
It's OK.
It's always OK.
And at those times when you think it's not OK, that's OK as well. It's OK not to be OK. Because that's OK as well.

Think about a fear you have. It's OK to have that fear. And in the moments you tell yourself that, the fear starts to reduce in power and release its grip over you. Got some strengths? That's OK. Got some weaknesses? That's OK as well. It's always OK because life always is. And that's OK as well. Unless you really and totally disagree with everything I am saying here.

And that's OK as well.

······
'YOU WERE BORN TO BE YOU, AND NO ONE ELSE.'
······

You may wonder whether, if someone says or does something that hurts you, is that OK? That is a big question that is very often asked, and it will be addressed later, in Truth 7. For now, just know that I don't believe that happiness, being centred and at peace mean the absence of problems, although what they do do is help you enormously with the ability to deal with those problems.

And you have a very simple action: because any, and every, time in the future that you touch your left thumb and first finger together, you will feel an immediate sense of joy, peace and self-assurance.

Like everything in the book, this is an incredibly powerful and effective, long-term method that works. They are all simple solutions, and that's why they work. As we've seen, the brain loves, adores, and opens itself to simple things.

When all the complexity, mystery and myths about this life are stripped away, we arrive at the very source of your happiness, your confidence and your peace. And that source is you – it always has been and always will be.

It's like you have often wanted to be somewhere else,

at some time else, and someone else, but wherever you go, there you are.

And yet, here you are – right here, right now.

······

'WHEREVER YOU GO, THERE YOU ARE.'

······

REMEMBER

Many people will inspire you to be the very best that you can be; others will tell you to be more than what you have become; this book invites you to be something totally different – to be the very best that you already are.

> You may have noticed that, as you read those words again – be the very best that you already are – you are feeling a warm energy flow through your mind, body and spirit.

And if that isn't the very definition of authenticity, then I don't know what is. Welcome to happiness, success and peace from a very different perspective – yours.

You. You were born to be you, and no one else, and that is all you ever need to be.

TRUTH 3

......

LOVE IS YOUR KILLER APP

••••••

When you are truly living, in a way that is driven by your self, you will know it, totally. If you 'get' that at a self level, you will know, behave and live with very high self-esteem, a good self-image and self-worth. You will be your own best friend, and believe that you are the 'finished article'. You will feel complete and overflowing. You will have so much to share that you give and throw out unconditional love to anyone and everyone you meet.

You will know that other people's success is not your failure. You are so calm, at peace and confident within yourself that you know you have everything you need to be happy. You never have to 'take' from anyone else. You live, instead of preparing to live. You give unconditional love not only to others but also and especially to yourself. You never need to be 'right' and you never need to talk about yourself because you truly know it's not about you; it's always about them.

••••••

'YOU GET UNCONDITIONAL LOVE BY GIVING IT.'

••••••

And when you go to bed, exhilarated, all the absolute uncon-ditional love comes back to you and fills your heart, one hundredfold.

When you merely exist, driven by your ego, you will know, behave and live with very low self-esteem, and have a poor self-image and self-worth. You will be your own worst enemy and believe you have 'something missing'. You will feel as if there is a hole in your heart and you will seek to fill that hole by taking from other people, which you do by putting them down, either to their face or stabbing them in the back.

You believe that other people's failure is your success, but this is no more than temporary. You are unsure, if not upset, about anyone and everyone you meet, including and especially yourself. You always need to be 'right'. You need to constantly talk about yourself because you need reassurance, admiration and respect from strangers. And when you go to bed, exhausted, fear, stress and unhappiness haunt you and empty out what little strength you have left.

Your attitude – your choice

In very simple terms, if people truly loved themselves they wouldn't have to *make* themselves the centre of everything, because they would know that they *are* the centre of every-thing.

A tree doesn't have to keep telling everyone that it's a tree – it knows it is a tree.

The reality is that we will always face issues, challenges and difficulties in our lives – we will all have 'bad' days and 'good' days. This book just serves to ensure that you will have many more of the wonderful moments, minutes, hours and days. It equips you with practical tips that you can apply straight away to help you overcome, deal with and move forward from any challenges you might face. This book will ensure that the vast majority of your life is lived as was intended on the day you were born – living, instead of preparing to live.

Your moments, your feelings, your attitude, your life, your future and your destiny do not come down to chance or change. They come down to choice, and that choice is yours. Always. It's not about you, and when you realize that, it *will* be all about you because when you focus on helping, loving and being kind to others you truly discover yourself.

If you stab, blame someone or hold other people accountable for how they 'make you feel' then in those moments you are, in effect, handing over your life to that person. You are handing over ownership of your choices and your precious moments. It's as if that person is more important in deciding your life than you are.

True humility, peace and love for yourself are all about showing true humility, peace and love for others. It can only ever happen when you do this. It's important to realize also that false humility is not humility at all. Many people who go on and on about being humble, shouting about how humble they are, are really so humble that they are on the point of self-destruction.

And, again, I exaggerate this for a reason – because the speed, stress and challenges of modern life take their toll on happiness. And we must help everyone with this situation, no matter how they act towards us.

......

'WHEN YOU FOCUS ON HELPING, LOVING
AND BEING KIND TO OTHERS
YOU TRULY DISCOVER YOURSELF.'

......

Be your own best friend

You will achieve 'wellness' in only one way: by being your own best friend. Love, respect and friendship are not mirrors of yourself; they are the source within you. When you love yourself, you will attract love from others. When you respect yourself, you magnetize respect from others, and when you are friendly to others – imagine being so right now to someone in your life – the friendship floods through you in return. In short – treat people the way you want them to be, and they will be, including, and especially, yourself.

I have always thought that the worst place to go when you are feeling ill is the doctor's, where everyone sits around spreading and receiving bugs. Fortunately these days, much of the health agenda centres on preventing physical and mental ill health, and my purpose here is to open up your mind to the possibility that within us, right now, we have the capacity to radically improve our wellbeing.

There are many physical things that we can do to improve our wellbeing, such as breathing properly, relaxation and meditation. That's all good stuff. Yet the most powerful way is simply to:

- be your own best friend
- love yourself unconditionally
- love everything you are – your gifts, your talents, your personality and your 'faults'.

Now there may be some negative thoughts that rush into your mind right now:

- 'That sounds pretty arrogant…'
- 'That's very big-headed.'
- 'How selfish would that make me?'

However, I am not talking about shouting from the rooftops 'Hey, look at me, I'm fantastic!' That's what we do if and when we need others to tell us we are great. I am also not talking about being defensive when someone 'attacks' us by something they say or do. That's what we do if and when we need to prove that we are 'right' and they are 'wrong'.

What I am talking about is simply admitting to ourselves what we already know and have always known: that we are unique, amazing and wonderful. And we do this by *showing* others this, each and every day, by our actions and by who we are.

This comes when you simply love yourself, without condition, always.

If you are not your own best friend, and do not love yourself, no one else will, because you won't let them. And you will be unable to love others or put other people first. Because you will be unsure of your own worth, you will feel the need to keep stealing from others. When you love yourself, you have no need to steal, because you will know that you are more than enough.

WORKSHOP:
Boost self-esteem

How to assess someone's self-esteem (without them knowing)

First, pay them a compliment and make it a genuine one. To truly assess their self-esteem, pay them three over the course of a conversation, for example:

- 'This is delicious - you are an amazing cook.'
- 'You must have a great memory.'
- 'Wow, you tell great stories.'

Now, they may block, ignore or deflect your compliments. They may even laugh nervously. If they do, their self-esteem is in need of a boost. It means that they do not feel a great sense of self-worth, so it is not possible for them to allow in such a feeling from someone else – they have to feel it for themselves first, to even know what it is.

And this is how to do it. Ask them helpful questions, as I showed you in the previous truth:

- 'Please share with us how you make such delicious...'
- 'What do you put your great memory down to?'
- 'How do you manage to tell such great stories?'

If this person's self-esteem is particularly low, their ego may again block, deflect or ignore. Nevertheless, they are far more likely to accept a compliment posed as a question than as a statement. Ultimately, though, a compliment can only ever be accepted by the person receiving it.

How to accept a genuine compliment
Now let's get back to how *you* should accept a compliment. First, look the person who paid you the compliment directly in the eye with warmth, kindness and gratitude, and say very simply, 'Thank you.'
Those two words are very important and play a big part in your life. Just by saying 'Thank you' to yourself, in silence,

can make you feel warm and glowing with sensations of tingling that run throughout your entire body. These are entirely natural feelings to experience right now. You will find that you feel altogether more at ease, more comfortable, more your self, than you did before you said it.

Strangely enough, accepting a compliment will have a similar profound effect on the person 'paying' it as it does for you. If, on the other hand, you don't accept it, you are in effect saying: 'Your opinions don't matter to me, and I don't think you are being genuine.'

How to accept a compliment you do not believe is genuine

This is a very clever and cunning technique for dealing with a compliment that you do not believe is genuine. Look the person saying it right in the eye, smile and say very simply, 'Thank you.'

In all situations, the 'Thank you' is a win_win: if the compliment was genuinely meant, all is well with both of you. If the compliment was not genuine, the person who paid it will look confused. Well done; you have managed to play with their head and given them something to think about without hurting them at all.

Be yourself – everyone else is already taken

Be yourself – your true, unlimited self, every day. You may as well be – after all, you spend 24 hours a day, 7 days a week, 52 weeks a year with yourself. You may as well get on, with you.

Be yourself and, in doing so, inspire and encourage other people to be themselves, too – their real, authentic, unlimited selves. Please spread the word that it's OK for them to be the very best that they already are, that there is nothing 'wrong' with them, that what they *can* do in life far outweighs what they *can't*.

Everyone has value. We should value everyone's different purposes, passions and personalities. We should value their opinions, thoughts and, above all, their story. Taking time to listen to someone else's stories, and I mean really listening, is the biggest single compliment we can ever pay another human being.

Have you ever wondered what that must be like, to be so calm, certain and self-confident that you can give and be yourself totally, without fear? Have you ever had that feeling? Focus your awareness on that idea for just a few moments and, as soon as you do, you will notice feelings of love coming from deep within you, because true love comes from within, not from without.

Here's how to never worry about what other people think of you, ever again (while being extremely popular!):

1. Give total and unconditional love to anyone and everyone that you ever meet, including and especially yourself.

2. Do not compare yourself to others.

3. Take total ownership of how you act, and react.

......

'GIVE TOTAL AND UNCONDITIONAL LOVE TO ANYONE AND EVERYONE YOU EVER MEET, INCLUDING AND ESPECIALLY YOURSELF.'

......

How to show love

I believe you can always tell someone's character by how nice they are to people they don't have to be nice to, as well as how they treat themselves. Here's how to show love for others:

- Be nice to people you don't have to be nice to. That includes waiters, reception staff, strangers who speak to you, and so on.

- Send only positive texts, emails and social media posts. Reply to negative ones you receive with positive responses.

- When someone you love, in your family or a friend, is negative towards you, remember that this is not about you. It is about where they are and what they are feeling at this moment in time. Do not respond as you might normally do, defensively, as this will not achieve the outcome you want.

- When someone is speaking, listen. Really listen – without judgement. It is perhaps the biggest single compliment we can ever pay another person.

- Don't think about what others think of you – think about what you think of them, and think highly of them, anyway.

- Smile!

This whole approach can be summarized simply by the quote on the next page.

'GO OUT LOOKING FOR FRIENDS AND YOU WILL FIND VERY FEW. GO OUT AND BE A FRIEND, AND YOU WILL FIND MANY.'

Here's how to show love for yourself:

- Just truly love yourself – *everything* about yourself.

- Accept compliments and feedback of all kinds with love and by saying 'Thank you.'

- Focus all your time on helping, praising and guiding others.

From now on, you will know it's not about you. It never has been and never will be. By loving yourself people will see you as strong, a leader and an inspiration. And when you are an inspiration, others are inspired. When you lead in this way, there is no need to tell others that you are their leader; you and they will know by who you are, what you say and what you do. Above all else, others will respect and like you.

Here's a test: at your next dinner party, meeting or social gathering, see if you can go for two hours without talking about yourself.

Try one hour.

Maybe even just 15 minutes.

OK – too long? OK, if all you do with the next person you meet for the first time is spend just three minutes asking them questions about themselves, and you really listen and repeat back what they are saying in your own words, they would not only like you – they would adore you, worship you, they would want to have your children.

It's simple, but it's not easy. All the time, your ego will be yelling in your head 'What about me?' or 'Anyway, enough about me, let's talk about you – what do you think about me?'

A positive attitude towards others, of simple, genuine, total interest in them, is contagious – it rubs off on others, and their behaviour, attitudes and life will change to match. They will like you, they will speak highly of you and they will think you are a friend, even if they have discovered absolutely nothing about you!

Please, always know this: every time your ego kicks in and you are aware of it, simply breathe, know it's OK and touch your thumb and first finger, and your self will come along. You breathe easily and slightly more slowly – your blood pressure lowers. Just as it did, then. Just as it is, now…

Do not compare yourself to others

Our brain, on its constant quest to preserve energy and keep us alive, loves to do things super-fast. And one aspect of doing things quickly is that, in order to determine the meaning of something, the brain compares new things to something it is already familiar with. And so, when it comes to success and what that means, we compare ourselves to others. If you think about it, this is a classic example of emotion winning over logic. That's because judging our own success against the success of others is unhelpful, inaccurate and, please forgive me, mad.

When you were born, did your parents benchmark you against all the other children in the neighbourhood? No, of course they didn't – well, not for a few years at least! And then you took over and regularly compared your success with that of others. It's tough to stop playing the comparison game, no matter what we learn, and so we continue buying stuff that we don't need, to impress people we have never met.

Not only do we often judge how successful we are by how successful other people are, it's even worse than that: we often judge how successful we are by how successful we *think* other people are. And, of course, we don't *know* how successful they are.

One thing I have discovered from meeting several celebrities and so-called 'successful' people is that they are just people – human beings, like the rest of us. Here's what I have learned: most celebrities I know don't actually have much money. They have limited freedom of speech, thought and action for fear that they will read about their exploits online within a few minutes of saying or doing it. Most disturbingly of all, they can't go out in the way you and I can. Can you imagine not being able to pop out to the local shop for some milk, for fear of being recognized, photographed or accosted?

This is not a dress rehearsal; you cannot rehearse being you. You *are* you, and you need to do this for those whose lives you touch, for your communities and organizations, and for your world.

> At times, it seems there is a taboo against being your own best friend, and as you read this it may feel as if that taboo is being lifted, out of you and high into the sky. Now imagine how it will feel when the taboo is gone. It's OK to be your own best friend – and, of course, it's OK not to be. Either way, if you think about those two alternatives, you *will* be your own best friend and return to being yourself. Welcome back!

Owning your actions and reactions

We always have total ownership and choice over what we think, say and do. Actually, let's stick with 'say and do' for now – but by the time you have completed this book 'think' will also be within your control.

We choose the words we use and we choose what actions we take. However, we cannot choose what words other people use, or what other people do. There are millions of things that go on around us that we cannot influence – such as weather, traffic, trains, news, holidays and so on. However, we can always choose how we react. That is always within our own gift, choice and control. And when we realize that, everything changes – from the quality of our emails and texts to the quality of our lives. Because what it means is that ultimately we have total ownership of how we act, and how we react – which is pretty much everything.

The idea that we always have total control over what we choose to do is such a powerful one that it might take a few moments to sink in. I know it did with me when I first discovered it. The realization for me came slowly and gradually. Perhaps it is the same for you, especially if you like to think things through for yourself.

I find that this idea transcends analysis. I suppose our minds can accept anything we can imagine when we know it will help our lives. And just by imagining whatever you are imagining, and whether you agree with having this degree of total freedom, your thoughts and analysis are perhaps little bubbles, bursting in your mind. And just as each one pops, you breathe slightly more deeply, from a calmer place.

Perhaps we can remove our biggest worry – the one that holds us back – which is about what other people think of us, on both a logical ego level and on an emotional self level.

The simple truth – a fact, even – is that other people don't spend that much time thinking or talking about you. They are too busy worrying what you and others think of them. With total respect and love, get over yourself. The only time people will be guaranteed to speak highly of you is when you are born and when you die.

......

'WE ALWAYS HAVE TOTAL OWNERSHIP AND CHOICE OVER WHAT WE THINK, SAY AND DO.'

......

You also need to remember that, no matter how other people behave towards you, whatever they say and do, it does not mean that you need to respond in kind. You can see how responding in kind is a bad idea by just looking at a couple of examples:

1. Emails: because they have no tone, emails can be a challenge and so we have to guess at the emotions behind the words, and therefore the meaning. Yet no email, text or word has any meaning other than the meaning that you choose to give to it. You know how it works – you respond to a negative email, or an email you perceive as negative, in a similarly negative way, and so the spiral begins, down and down. And when you respond to a perceived negative email positively, the spiral begins, up and up.

2. Texts: I once received a text from the chairman of an event I was due to speak at the next day. 'Hi David, look forward to seeing you tomorrow. I hear you are a good speaker, although you do have a lot to learn.' At this point, my ego kicked in and started to get angry. I had given the email the only meaning it could possibly have – that was now the meaning, the truth – and when the ego mind believes something to be true, the self makes it true. And then I thought, 'OK, David, practise what you preach…', and I replied: 'Thank you, looking forward to it and yes, I do have a lot to learn. See you on Tuesday.' To which he replied: 'Yes, I am so impressed that you are not using any notes or PowerPoint and are learning the whole thing off by heart.'

That is not to say that sometimes people are not angling to have a go at you. For example, I was once mentoring a young girl in the Prince's Trust, a charity that helps young people overcome huge difficulties they have had in their lives. She sent me a text late one evening. It read:

'You are a coward.'

I knew that text was not about me – it was about her. I called her straight away, and, sure enough, she needed my help.

Next time someone does that to you, remember that it is about them, not you. And if you get upset, that is your choice. Just remember that getting upset is unhelpful and will not put you in a place that will help you respond in a way that will help you both.

Being your true self

The word 'selfish' is a confusing one. We think that if someone is selfish they are thinking only about themselves. However, if we choose to be our true selves, we will often demonstrate the opposite and become suddenly totally selfless.

When you are in this state of mind, body and spirit, you will know it. You will:

- help other people every day – opportunities to do this will present themselves to you automatically as you live your life

- feel wonderful 24/7 – you will go around with a grin on your face and other people won't know why

- lose arguments and be happy to do so – especially at home with your family.

You will also find that every day you come from a place of love, and never fear or hate. You will send out radiance, warmth and love to everyone you meet. You will do this when you are talking to people face to face, on the phone or by email. And when you are in conversation, you will always talk about the other person's favourite subject – themselves. This is the most amazing change that being in this state will do for you.

This does not mean giving in to others or that you will never make mistakes or do things you later regret, but it does mean that from this moment on you will never again have any fears about whether you are liked by other people, because it won't matter. You love yourself, and the love you subsequently attract from all around you will keep you overflowing for the rest of your existence.

Other people will like you anyway, because you will be so sure of your true self and have such genuine care and compassion for others, always putting them first.

And then you will know, it's not about you.

It's never about you.

And that's OK.

......

'IF YOU COME FROM A PLACE OF LOVE, YOU WILL SEND OUT RADIANCE, WARMTH AND LOVE TO EVERYONE YOU MEET.'

......

The killer app

Our daughter Olivia was seven years old and she was lying in bed, doing everything she could think of to avoid going to sleep.

OLIVIA: I don't have enough love to give to everyone.
ME: What do you mean?
OLIVIA: Well, I have 100 per cent of love, and I don't have enough love to go around. *[She then allocated percentages of love to various family members and then concluded, rather sadly.]* So I don't have enough love for the cats or the goldfish. *[And not very much for me, I thought; however, I let that pass.]* Daddy, I don't have enough love to give to everyone.

I gave her a big cuddle, and said that love doesn't work like percentages – how you can give 100 per cent of love to one person and also 100 per cent to another. Love is without limit and the more you give away, the more you get back in return. She calmed down and closed her eyes.

OLIVIA: OK.
ME: Love is the killer app – hey, I might use that in a book one day.
OLIVIA: *[eyes still closed and now completely calm]* I wouldn't if I were you.'

TRUTH 4

......

REALITY IS WHAT YOU MAKE IT

• • • • • •

We make up our own realities – we live in worlds of our own based on the meaning we give, or attach, to every single event, thought and moment. We all see the world through different lenses, and that means that you can choose how you see things. We don't see things as they are – we see things as we are.

Let's see how this might work in action.

Two shoe salespeople from different companies travel to a far-flung country to assess the market situation. After just a day, the first salesperson contacts his manager to say, 'They have never even heard of shoes here, let alone worn them… I'm heading back home on the next flight.'

The second salesperson also contacts his manager to say, 'They have never even heard of shoes here, let alone worn them… Send me everything you've got.'

Here's another one. Look at this sentence:

'I didn't say she stole the money.'

Now try rereading that simple sentence with a different emphasis on each word in turn. Every time you change the emphasis, the whole sentence gains a completely different meaning.

••••••

`WE DON'T SEE THINGS AS THEY ARE – WE SEE THINGS AS WE ARE.´

••••••

Now let's look at a word. Let's look at:

Failure

Have a go at defining that one word for yourself. Everyone will come up with a different definition, depending on their individual experience and view of the world. Some definitions may be similar to others, but each one will be slightly different.

Failure is a noun. And in that four-letter word comes the moment of infinite possibilities because, with nouns, we make up the meaning we give them. Samuel Johnson did just that, many years ago, when he decided what each word meant for his famous dictionary. If he can do it, so can you. He won't mind; he has been dead for over 250 years.

My definition of failure, for example, is that it is one of the most exciting things of all, because it helps me discover how not to do something, and that is absolutely essential on the road to success. That is why I kept all the rejection

• • • • • •

'"WHEN I USE A WORD," HUMPTY DUMPTY
SAID, IN A RATHER A SCORNFUL TONE,
"IT MEANS JUST WHAT I CHOOSE IT
TO MEAN — NEITHER MORE NOR LESS."

"THE QUESTION IS," SAID ALICE,
"WHETHER YOU CAN MAKE WORDS
MEAN SO MANY DIFFERENT THINGS."

"THE QUESTION IS," SAID HUMPTY
DUMPTY, "WHICH IS TO BE
MASTER — THAT'S ALL."'

• • • • • •

Lewis Carroll, *Alice through the Looking-Glass* (1872)

letters I received when I applied to write my first magazine column – a total of 47 (yes, in those days, letters!). I loved every one of them because I always got up again after the initial disappointment and learned to do something different. My only regret is that they finally said 'yes' at 48 because I was looking forward to 50 – I had a special bottle of champagne ready for that one.

And so 'failure' is what you define it to be. It is your reality, your choice. Please choose wisely!

Let's define another word:

Happiness

For me, I always feel happy when I am above ground and breathing. That is my rule. And therefore I am always happy (except in the subway).

Almost all words have multiple meanings. My personal favourite is 'communication', because in organizations almost every staff survey concludes that 'communication' needs to improve. The challenge is that many people will have a completely different definition of what they mean by the term 'communication'. I believe that word has so many meanings that it has become virtually meaningless. How ironic is that?

The idea is not to redefine each word in the dictionary, but to give each word a meaning, to ourselves, that helps us.

Just like Humpty Dumpty in *Alice through the Looking-Glass*, we do it anyway so we may as well do it in a way that helps. And it's not just words; it's also events and the different meanings we give to them.

Imagine you are sitting on a plane, waiting to take off. You are relaxed and reading a book. Just behind you, a man is clearly very nervous – almost petrified. He is clearly not looking forward to flying and the fuss he is making is threatening to delay take-off.

What is the difference between you and him? It's not the reality – you are both on the same plane, in the same type of seat, at exactly the same time. No, it's the perception – how you are both choosing to react to the situation.

And the ultimate thing we make up is time itself. Time is relative – it is not an absolute – which is why:

- those five minutes in the dentist's chair seem so much longer than those five minutes being with someone you love.

- that minute added on at the end of the game passes so much more quickly when you are losing than when you are winning

- we literally made up all measurement systems, the time zones and everything to do with them.

Your future – your choice

It is humans who label things and give things meaning. Then we say that's the way things actually are. What happens next is entirely up to you, always.

We always have total control and ownership of what we say and do – and how we act. We don't always have control of what other people say and do – and how they act. We do, however, always have control of how we react – not just to what other people say and do but also to events, to emails, to the weather and so on. And when we take control – with 100-per-cent ownership of how we react, we can react in a way that takes us closer to our outcome, not further away.

A project goes wrong and while everyone else in the meeting is looking for someone to blame, you can say, 'How does this going wrong help us get this project live on time?'

You always have control over how you act, and react.

THE CIRCLE OF REALITY

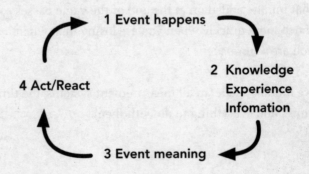

1 Event happens

2 Knowledge Experience Infomation

3 Event meaning

4 Act/React

When something happens, we start the the 'circle of reality':

- **Stage 1:** An event happens – it can be a thought, something said or something done. To protect our energy, our ego immediately asks, what does this event mean?

- **Stage 2:** To answer that question, we look at our past knowledge (everything we have learned), our experiences (everything that has happened to us) and our imagination. And of these three areas, which one 'wins' in terms of being the biggest factor in determining the meaning? It's imagination every time, and by a clear margin. That's because in that moment we cannot remember every piece of knowledge that we have amassed, and we cannot recall all of our experiences, and so for the missing bits we make it up and then we react.

- **Stage 3:** That determines the meaning we give to the event.

- **Stage 4:** And we act/react accordingly, which is, of course, another event, and around we go again – round and round, hundreds of times a day, thousands of times a week, millions of times a year.

We will revisit the circle later – to show how we can be in control of our own thoughts, meanings and reactions, rather than the other way around.

······

'WE AUTOMATICALLY MOVE IN THE DIRECTION OF OUR DOMINANT THOUGHTS.'

······

Our minds automatically move in the direction of our most dominant thoughts. What we think about defines what we become. To see this work for yourself, try this experiment.

WORKSHOP: The pendulum

Whenever your mind focuses exclusively on a single thought or idea, your body responds.

To do this, you will need to make a simple pendulum by obtaining a piece of string and tying a heavy object to one end.

1. Hold the top end of pendulum between thumb and forefinger, with the weight at the bottom.
2. Keep your hand still. Feel it getting still.
3. Close your eyes (but read the rest of the instructions first!).

4. In your mind, think of the pendulum swinging back and forth. Picture it; visualize it purely in your mind. In your mind, picture it moving backwards and forwards. Back and forth.

5. All the time, keep your hand completely still. Do this in your mind for about a minute, and then open your eyes.

You will find that the pendulum is swinging from side to side. The larger the swing, the bigger your thought and picture. This shows how your mind wants to help you. How the experiment works is that the movement is caused by involuntary muscle movements in the hand, induced by your own mental processes, where your thoughts and ideas cause tiny micro-muscular movements to occur. These are picked up and amplified by the pendulum to produce this astonishing effect.

When we believe something to be true, we see the world that way

At the beginning of this chapter I explained how we interpret events to support what we believe. This ties into our self's role in supporting whatever our ego is thinking.

WORKSHOP: **What's reality?**

This experiment illustrates how our minds cannot tell the difference between something that happens in 'reality' and something we imagine with emotional intensity.

1. Stand up, and point directly in front of you with your right or left arm.
2. With your feet and legs staying as they are, and twisting your waist, move your right arm to the right, left arm to the left, round and behind your body. Move your arm as far as you can, and see how far it goes.
3. Note the point, and return your arm to your side.
4. Now close your eyes and imagine doing the same thing but keep your arms physically by your side: in your mind, point your arm out in front of you, then move it round to the right or left, as you did in reality before.
5. As you reach the point you reached just now, you will find that something extraordinary happens, because then, easily, effortlessly and automatically, your arm travels another six, maybe nine, maybe 12 inches – 20 centimetres – maybe even more. As you do this now, see just how much farther you can imagine your arm going around.

6. Now repeat what you have just imagined, for real: once again, point directly in front of you with your right or left arm.

7. With your feet and legs staying as they are, and twisting on your waist, move your right arm to the right, left arm to the left, round and behind your body.

8. This time you will find that your arm will go way past the point it reached the first time, and probably as far, if not farther, than you imagined.

You are always, always, capable of far more than you may believe. And the way to prove that is to believe it. So many people say, 'I'll believe it when I see it.' Now, you may choose to say: 'I'll see it when I believe it.'

Your reality – your life – your choice

Is this headline true?

'Yes, because, as a human being, I agree that we make up our own reality. We make up our own realities about words, events and with anything that we imagine. All our reactions, our opinions, our beliefs – in short, our truths – come down to this. It is always our choice.'

'No, because, as a human being, I don't agree that we make up our own reality. We don't make up our own realities about words, events and with anything that we imagine.'

'Sorry, David, I don't agree with you, and so my reality is different from yours…'

'Ah – I see that it's true because I don't believe that it's true – we have made different choices, proving that our belief, reality and life is our choice.'

Mind the Gap

This is not the gap between platform and underground train, but the Gap of Infinite Possibility. It's the place where your future, your life and what happens to you next are totally and absolutely within your own control, and no one else's.

Please just reflect on that for a moment. Thank you. That is all you get, though – a single moment.

Yes, the Gap is amazingly empowering and powerful – it is also, rather short. Still, the good news is that, with practice, you can be aware of it and make it a little bit longer.

The Gap changes everything because it allows us – you, me, anyone – to choose a different meaning for any event.

THE GAP IN THE CIRCLE OF REALITY

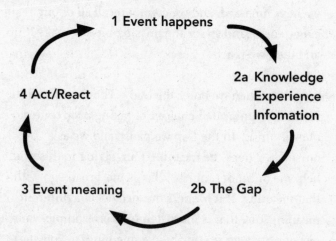

As before, when something happens we start the the 'circle of reality':

- **Stage 1:** An event happens – it can be a thought, something said or something done. To protect our energy, our ego immediately asks, what does this event mean?

- **Stage 2a:** To answer that question, we look at our past knowledge (everything we have learned), our experiences (everything that has happened to us) and our imagination. And of these three areas, which one 'wins' in terms of being the biggest factor in determining the meaning? It's imagination every time, and by a clear margin. That's because in that moment we cannot remember every piece of knowledge that we have amassed, and we cannot recall all of our experiences, and so for the missing bits we make it up and then we react.

- **Stage 2b:** Then we enter the Gap – The Gap of Infinite Possibility, unlimited choices, of taking back control of everything. In the Gap we pause and we ask ourselves – does the meaning I am giving to this event help me or hinder me? If it helps me, great – go with that meaning. If it hinders me, decide on a different meaning, one that is more helpful. For example, your partner has a go at you about something, so you start round the circle and are about to dismiss what he/she says as trivial, when you stop in the Gap and say to yourself something like: 'Hang on, if I treat this comment as trivial we are going to have one almighty row. It is important to my partner, whom I love, so it must be important to me.'

- **Stages 3 and 4:** And so you give the event a totally different meaning and you complete the circle.

······

'THIS THING WE CALL LIFE HAS WHATEVER MEANING YOU CHOOSE TO GIVE IT.'

······

Here is another example of not entering and entering the Gap.

Say it's just started to rain. You might think, 'It's starting to rain, that's really bad news, so much for my weekend plans of doing the garden!'

Or you might think, 'It's starting to rain, that's really good news, it means the dry period is over – the grass and plants really need it – I can't wait for the weekend to do the garden!'

I know that we have to give things in life a meaning – if we didn't, we wouldn't be able to function. All I'm saying is that we have the ability to choose our own meanings. In the example above, the only indisputable fact and reality is that it's starting to rain. Other than that fact, the rest of the interpretation is for us to choose, know, and decide.

The Gap is the moment to be aware, alert and alive to, to take a little pause, let time stand still and assess the most useful meaning, before consciously deciding on the most appropriate and useful response. It is the Gap of Infinite Possibility, because that is what you have. Be aware of the Gap and it will grow in length, choices and power.

- You might decide to wake up in the morning and decide the day ahead means that everything will go well for you; that everything everyone says around you will be positive. Now watch what happens.

- Or maybe you take it one stage further and decide that every single event that happens in your life helps take you closer to achieving your dream, outcome or goal. Then experience what happens.

This thing we call life, then, has whatever meaning you choose to give it. Please choose wisely what meaning you give it – make it a meaning that helps you and those whose lives you touch.

If you are feeling brave, and want to discover a place of perfect harmony, decide that anything and everything that happens to you, or around you, or within you, actually helps you. Everything. Including these words right now. Ask yourself each and every day, how does this event, this person, this day, help me to achieve my outcome? And how does this moment help me to help someone else to achieve their outcome?

How does that make you feel? Perhaps all the stress you felt seems like it is in the past, way back, behind you.

TRUTH 5

••••••

YOU CAN SILENCE
YOUR EGO VOICE

• • • • • •

You know the voice I mean – it's the one that tells you every day that you are not good enough, that you are not worthy of success and that you have a lot to worry about. In short, it says that you have done wrong, are doing wrong and will do wrong. It sometimes disguises itself as a softer voice. Right now, for example, you might be thinking, 'He's going on about that voice again – enough already, David.'

That's the one – the one that just said that to you. Don't be fooled by its disguises: it's the same voice, the one now on high alert, which tells us that we are wrong across the whole of our lives. All through the life we have lived up to this moment, the regretful voice has replayed what we have done wrong. This, when you think about it, is not very helpful, as the past has passed. It is not as if the voice provides us with a time machine in which to travel back and do something differently.

For the life we have yet to live, our future, the judging voice will already be telling us what we may yet do wrong, before we even have a chance to do it. You may have a dream, a new idea, an ambition, and this voice will enter your head more quickly than lightning with its eternal question, 'How are you going to do that?' And when you respond with, 'I don't know,' it will tell you, 'If you don't know how, then you can't achieve it.'

This is why it is so critical to separate the 'what' and the 'how'.

Next time the voice says asks, 'How are you going to do that?' respond with, 'I don't know, yet.' As you read those four words again, you will mentally feel the 'what' and the 'how' drifting apart, separating, leaving you with a new fire, hope and enthusiasm to go for it.

Very soon the voice will go silent. Yes, that private, internal, infernal voice that you may have had for most of your life will simply go quiet, dissolve and disappear.

What will it be like when that inner voice is no longer judging you, telling you off, keeping you back from your dreams? Just imagine now that it is already happening. Its power over you is reducing in size, so it is no longer over you, it's beside you, separate from you, still close, until it's outside you, some distance away. It's as if you are floating on a cloud. Can you feel a sense of comfort growing? Imagine now the most tranquil, peaceful, beautiful scene, with you at the very centre.

The second main purpose of the ego is to stop you taking risks or opportunities, saying what you truly believe in case you are shouted down, or going for your dreams in case you feel and look stupid in the future. And it then helpfully paints a strong, vivid and real picture in your mind (remember the mind can't tell the difference between what happens in reality and what it imagines with emotional intensity), which is more than strong enough for you to stop thinking about it.

And the really strange, illogical part of this is obvious: the future – your future – has not even happened yet. Unlike the past, you can actually shape, design and influence your own future. The ego, though, is scared by that idea, and so it talks you out of doing something, long before you haven't actually done it.

The ultimate trick we play on ourselves through our ego is that it convinces us that the Now doesn't exist. How can we possibly live in it or experience it, when it is some kind of elusive fiction? And it is this dark, black magic trick that has caused us all to keep looking for something that we actually already have within us. Recently, it has even led to a huge increase in the sales of Mind, Body and Spirituality books and self-help books, signified by an outbreak of 'mind-fulness' books.

Ego: the imaginary voice

I want to share with you a simple truth: *this annoying, relentless and unforgiving voice is not real – it is imaginary.* And imaginary voices, fears and feelings call for imaginary solutions. If you have wanted to get rid of this voice for years, what have you actually done about it to date?

There are four main strategies that people tell me about (numbers three and four are the most common):

1. **They distract it.** They start thinking about a new subject in the mistaken belief that this will work. It doesn't – all that happens is that the voice simply transfers itself to your new train of thought, whatever it is. Come on, do you think it would be that easy? Let's not forget who you are taking on here – yourself.

2. **They ignore it.** Again, this is great in principle: ignore it and move on. But how can you do that? The very voice that is shouting 'Ignore me!' is the voice itself or, if it's by chance the self-voice whispering something positive, you simply can't ignore it unless you are asleep, hypnotized, or truly living in this very moment.

3. **They tell it to go away.** They do this perhaps by convincing it, and yourself, that what the voice says is wrong.

4. **They argue with it.** They hope to convince it (and you) that what it is saying is wrong.

Now, because these are the most frequent actions that people take to quieten their personal voice, you might think they are the most effective. Wrong.

Have you ever experienced the following? You are lying in bed, trying to sleep, replaying the events of the day. The first sign of the voice, especially at night, is not in the mind, it is in the gut. It feels like a hard body blow that sends shivers down your spine and fear into your whole being. The thought of sleep now seems way off in the distance…

You think: 'I wouldn't have normally said that. Why did you? It was obviously a stupid thing to say… Did you notice the way people reacted when you said it? What are you, some kind of imbecile?'

You reason with yourself, you talk, discuss and argue with yourself, in silence or maybe even out loud.

How many people do you need in a room to have a disagreement? Many would answer 'Two'. A psychologist would answer 'One'. And the psychologist is right – it just takes you and your ego chatting away as if your happiness depended on it, which, of course, it does.

Your happiness, your confidence and your lack of stress depend on you winning the argument as you lie in bed. And you get about halfway there. You convince yourself that the email you received from your boss wasn't that bad, it didn't really mean what you thought it did, and that all is well in the world. Finally, exhausted, you fall asleep. In the morning, when you wake up, your ego inner voice might immediately say to you:

'Good morning! You are still alive, let's rejoice in another wonderful day ahead. Oh, so you know, I'm still not sure that your boss's email was OK. Can we resolve this so that you can forget about it and enjoy your day?'

Unfortunately, what it actually does is hit you again in your stomach with the full force and worry of what happened the day before, the moment you wake up. It completely discounts all your hard work convincing yourself the night before. This doesn't seem fair, but the ego doesn't do fair or unfair – it simply protects, and often overprotects, us. This provides more evidence that, when it comes to reason and logic versus emotion and feelings, the latter wins, every time.

······

`THE EGO DOESN'T DO FAIR OR UNFAIR – IT SIMPLY PROTECTS, AND OFTEN OVERPROTECTS, US.`

······

Fighting with your ego not only never works but it also makes the ego voice so much stronger, and it is the only way its negative voice can exist. You will know from other parts of your life that fighting, arguing or disagreeing with something makes the problem bigger, whether it's with your partner, family, colleagues or, in this case, yourself.

A big question then, if none of these strategies work, is why people persist with them. It's because they don't know the following very simple, effective and powerful technique that always works. It will ensure that you are calm, centred and totally relaxed wherever you are, and whatever the time of day or night.

This technique is for yourself, and for your self – your Spiritual Everlasting Loving Friend. It will allow your self to come to the fore.

Quietening your ego voice – for ever

Everything in this chapter up until now was not just build-up; it was to get your ego on side and ready for this moment. Your ego is now ready if you are feeling slightly calmer than you did just a few moments ago.

Your ego would have found a lot of what I have written too obvious, repetitive and boring. And that is exactly what we wanted to happen. We need it to be on side – just as we need our ego in our life – but just not going on and on at us all the time.

We need a way, a how-to, a strategy that will quieten it whenever we choose. This will allow you to be in control of your ego rather than letting it be in control of you.

In a moment, you will be listening to your own unhelpful, ego voice and doing something very simple that will make it quieten, soften and melt away into silence. I give your ego chatter fair warning – you are about to be quietened. And perhaps you noticed then, or are noticing now, that the stronger those words sound, like they should be giving your fiery, negative ego voice more power, they are in fact giving it less power, and it is slightly weaker, and perhaps, even before we use the technique, you are now noticing it going quiet, or if not completely quiet, then certainly quieter still.

WORKSHOP:
How to quieten your ego

Wherever you are, please, right now, acknowledge your ego voice. And if you find yourself asking, 'What voice?' that's the one – the one that asked that very question! Listen to your ego voice chatting away.

1. And now, with total certainty, belief and love, say to yourself, in silence, 'Thank you.' And at the same time as you say it, breathe a long breath out and feel that breath dropping downwards, from your mouth

through your neck and past your stomach until you have fully breathed out.

2. And your voice will go quiet, it is going quiet and it has gone quiet.

3. Now breathe in.

4. And repeat the words, 'Thank you.'

5. Your voice will go quiet, it is going quiet and it has gone quiet.

Silence.

You may notice in the silence – as you listen to the silence itself – a very slight, quiet whisper entering your head. Cleared of your ego voice, your self voice is with you, within you, right now. It is soft, loving and kind. And it whispers to you, right now – very simply – 'I love you.'

······

'WITH TOTAL CERTAINTY, BELIEF
AND LOVE, SAY TO YOURSELF,
IN SILENCE, "THANK YOU".'

······

'Thank you' is, of course, a phrase made up of two simple words used to accept a compliment, spoken privately, warmly and silently. That's it.

Your blood pressure will have decreased: if you have one of those blood pressure apps, or watches, have a look and see. Your breathing and pulse rate will have slowed. That's right. Very good.

Truth 5 has taken our ego voice from annoying to discomfort to possibility to relaxation, to total surrender to absolute peace.

Time to reflect

All your inner voice has ever wanted is to be acknowledged, to be respected and to be loved.

Loved.

At this present moment – now – right now, you will be able to hear sounds around you, sights and wonders that perhaps you were not aware of before. Or maybe those you could hear before you now sense with a new clarity.

You are totally here and present and it is as if it is just you and me and no one else. And as soon as you notice that, the sooner your other voice emerges, your true self, and it whispers 'I love you.'

TRUTH 6

......

WHY YOU DO
WHAT YOU DO

• • • • • •

Please don't let the length of this chapter fool you. In talking about a Truth, less is very often more.

New Scientist famously once carried on its cover the sentence, 'The idea that human beings are rational is risible.' We may be irrational, and here's the rub: we are predictably irrational. As human beings, we will only ever do something to the best of our abilities for one reason, and one reason alone, and that is if we want to.

One of the biggest secrets of human behaviour is why human beings really do what they do. It's why you, your friends and family, and everyone on earth, really do what they do.

People will only ever do something to the very best of their abilities for one reason, and one reason alone, namely because they choose to. And they will do this on the basis of the choices they believe that have available to them at that moment – which are based entirely on their self-image – that will move them closer to pleasure and/or further away from pain.

Remember:

- You always have a choice. Often you have more choice than you may immediately realize. And when you have run out of choices, and all of them have been exhausted, please know this: you haven't.

- This book is all about your self-worth, self-esteem and self-confidence.

- 'Pain' and 'pleasure' exist by your own definition. If you really want the willpower to change something in your life, consider and ramp up the pain you will feel by not taking action, and do the same for the pleasure you will receive when you achieve your dream outcome.

And now you know why everyone – including you – does anything.

......

'OFTEN YOU HAVE MORE CHOICE THAN YOU MAY IMMEDIATELY REALIZE. AND WHEN YOU HAVE RUN OUT OF CHOICES, AND ALL OF THEM HAVE BEEN EXHAUSTED, PLEASE KNOW THIS: YOU HAVEN'T.'

......

WORKSHOP: **The eight secrets of happy children**

Here are some tips for parents and grandparents to help young people have higher self-esteem and therefore more choices.

1. Say 'yes' to your child as often as you say 'no'. Your child needs to know where he or she stands, not just where they fall. Do this one thing alone and your child will grow up with higher self-esteem.

2. Tell them you love them every single day, especially last thing before they go to sleep.

3. When you praise them, be specific about what the praise is for.

4. Encourage them how to think, not what to think – be careful about giving your opinions as if they are facts. And listen to what they say – really listen.

5. Play/be with them when they want you to – five minutes after doesn't work.

6. Remember that children are very clever and aware from the moment they are born, so never look down at them (indeed, when you speak to them, kneel to their level).

7. Show a genuine interest in an interest of theirs – be it a TV programme, book or hobby – and don't judge their choice of music as your parents may have judged yours. When you sit down to watch their favourite programme, they will show they love having you there by explaining about what is going on, who the characters are, and so on.

8. If your son or daughter says they want to be an astronaut or something similarly ambitious when they grow up, don't 'tell the truth' about how difficult that would be and explain the education, dedication and hard work needed. Just say, 'And you will be a very good astronaut.' They need to believe that anything's possible, and in any case tomorrow they may well want to be something different – and what right do we have to impose our limited beliefs on their dreams for the future?

TRUTH 7

......

WAR OR PEACE? THE CHOICE IS YOURS

• • • • • •

This Truth uses a mixture of ego-conscious and self-subconscious methods to create a cocktail of the most proven, practical and powerful techniques I have ever discovered. Based on what we have covered in the book so far, this will be a practical chapter on overcoming seven challenges, problems or wars that we fight within ourselves and with other people – sometimes at the same time!

It will give you a practical, real-world application. Or rather, it will give you a practical, your-world experience, unique to your own perceptions and the lens you use to see the world. With each solution I will also explain why it works.

The seven challenges I will teach you to overcome are these:

1. How to take the heat out of an argument
2. How to achieve success in the fastest way by far
3. How to remove a phobia
4. How to forgive
5. How to use your mind to control your body
6. How to make any change to your life in the fastest way possible
7. How to make peace with your parents – whether they are alive or not

1 Take the heat out of an argument

When you want to diffuse an argument or reduce someone's negative response to a conflict, you can change someone's state by using distraction – drawing their attention away from the situation they are in and the emotions they are attaching to that situation, by guiding their attention elsewhere. This distraction technique is one mastered by magicians; its impact is amazing.

My children Olivia and Anthony used to fight when they were young. One day, when Olivia was five, she came to me, very upset and angry. Just a year before, I probably would have said something like 'Calm down' or 'Stop crying', but these injunctions did not work.

I wanted to calm her down and deep down she wanted the same, even if she didn't realize it right then. However, she was so upset that she didn't know how to calm down.

ME: What's wrong?

OLIVIA: *[between angry crying]* Anthony hit me, and…

ME: *[interrupting her and pointing out of the window]* Hold on, Olivia, look at Arthur.

Arthur, one of our cats, was asleep just outside the window, in his favourite place – on the shed roof. Olivia stopped mid-sentence and looked, just for a second, before I said: 'Sorry, Olivia, you were saying?'

Olivia looked at me, confused, simply unable to find the levels of anger and fury that she felt just a few moments before – they had gone.

······

'YOU CAN CHANGE SOMEONE'S STATE BY USING DISTRACTION.'

······

WHY IT WORKS

The events that caused Olivia to feel so emotional – the argument with her brother – had reached their peak of impact when she came to see me. She was literally out of control, and being out of control was only making her feelings more intense (a major cause of stress is when we feel we are not in control). If I had talked with her about her feelings, or about the object of the argument, her brother, or the subject of the argument, those feelings would have continued. Distracting attention away from them dissipated them.

2 Achieve success in the fastest way by far

To be more successful, at something – fast – it is simply a matter of copying someone who has already achieved what you want to achieve, doing what they did. And that's it.

You can find out what they did simply by asking them. When you ask, make sure you use this phrase in your question: 'I would very much value your help, advice and guidance.' Then it's not cheating!

WHY IT WORKS
It gives you a great start on your journey to success. And, as you go on, inevitably you will stamp your own character, approach and ideas on it that will make it your own.

3 Remove a phobia

This technique, the 'Fast Fear and Phobia Cure', will successfully remove a phobia.

What are you scared of? I will pretend here that you are scared of spiders (as many of us are), but please substitute your own fear.

1. If you are scared of spiders, think of them now.
SPIDERS

2. You will feel that fear deep in the pit of your stomach. Close your eyes and feel it. It won't be still, or it would have no impact on you. The fear will have movement. Imagine this movement in your mind as large red arrows turning in circles. Notice whether the arrows are turning clockwise or anti-clockwise. Let's say that the feeling you have is very intense.

3. Now be ready for something that is so incredible and astonishing, it will feel almost like a magic trick. Now, right now, feel the movement slowing down... until the arrows stop.

4. See it, feel it. Imagine those arrows s l o w i n g d o w n ... until they stop and stay still within you.

5. Now, in an instant, turn those arrows from red to blue.

6. As soon as you focus on the stillness of the arrows, now a soft, comforting, natural blue, you will instantly feel a reduction in the strength, the stress and the hold of that fear. These changes do not take ages – you may well have developed your fear or phobia in a heartbeat, so it makes sense that it can be removed in a similar time period.

7. Now, picture, feel, and almost hear those beautiful blue arrows starting to move in the opposite direction, starting again very s l o w l y. They move round and round, not

too fast, not too slow, merely in perfect time, rhythm and harmony, at a speed that feels comfortable, comforting and right for you.

8. And as they move, and because of the way they are moving – their direction, their colour and their flow – all your previous, negative feelings have been replaced by even stronger feelings of being at one with yourself, the world and everyone in it. And that's OK.

And it's OK now.

WHY IT WORKS

Imaginary fears can be removed only with imaginary solutions. If something is causing you to feel bad, the opposite will very often give you the opposite effect. Remember, no matter what your fear or phobia, you did not have it on the day you were born (unless it's a fear of loud noises or falling). Its strength and hold over you depends on you fighting it. However, if you let it go and replace it with a more natural feeling, you return to being yourself, as you were on the day you were born. Yes, it's you, the real you. Just so.

······

'IMAGINARY FEARS CAN BE REMOVED ONLY WITH IMAGINARY SOLUTIONS.'

······

4 Forgive

I know from personal experience that forgiving others is one of the bravest, hardest, most emotional things we can ever do. If you want to forgive yourself and/or others, you can carry out a technique called Jingi, which leads to peace and forgiveness. The term 'Jingi' is Japanese and it has no direct English translation. For me, the closest words, feelings and meaning are humanity, redemption and peace with your self.

1. Find somewhere quiet to relax and be at peace. Cover yourself mentally with a purple cloak or curtain. Make the colour a very deep purple; make the cloak large and sweeping, and let it flow all over you. Breathe, relax and close your eyes.

2. Now allow the people whom you have argued with, fallen out with, hurt or been hurt by, to enter your mind, one by one. Perhaps start with a teacher from your school. Acknowledge them as they come into your mind, and look at them for a few seconds. They are some distance away from you, almost as if you are watching them on a cinema screen.

3. Now, let them go, see them walk away into the distance. You watch them on the screen, getting smaller and smaller, until they disappear from your mind for good.

And as you let them go, say to yourself, out loud or simply in your head, 'I choose peace over this.'

4. 'I choose peace over this.'

5. Notice, as you reread those five words and say them again – silently or out loud – to yourself, how you are gradually relaxing, as if a huge weight has been lifted off your shoulders.

Next, please find yourself remembering pleasant memories and let them form rapidly in your mind. You might want to stay with those heart-warming thoughts for a few moments, for as long as you choose. Would you prefer to stay with those uplifting feelings or simply to relax comfortably for the next few seconds?

......
'FORGIVING OTHERS IS ONE OF THE BRAVEST, HARDEST, MOST EMOTIONAL THINGS WE CAN EVER DO.'
......

WHY IT WORKS

This method is crammed full of techniques: placebos, association, disassociation, vivid imagination, replacing a negative with a positive, and all these techniques are stacked on top of one another.

5 Use your mind to control your body

My wife, Rosalind, and I have been married for more than 19 years, and not so long ago I had a real problem with our marriage: my wedding ring had become too tight or, as my daughter said, I had become 'too fat'. In any case, I needed to get it resized. Yet no matter what I did, I could not get the ring off. It was a 'Catch-22' as the fact that it was so tight was restricting the blood supply in my finger and causing the knuckle of my finger to swell even more.

People advised me to go to a jeweller to have it cut off. I researched this online, and other people's experiences of this procedure convinced me that having the ring cut off was the most dangerous thing in the world. What to do?

I made a true decision. I would get the ring off my finger myself using the power of my mind. I sat down and closed my eyes. I gently touched the ring with the thumb and third finger of my right hand. I imagined the ring was a screw and my right hand was a screwdriver, and at the same time I kept saying to myself, 'Very loose ring, very tiny finger.' With that I slowly unscrewed it.

As it reached my knuckle, my ego voice unhelpfully chimed in: 'Nope, that's not going to come off at all.' I thanked the voice and it dissolved, replaced with an absolute certainty that the ring was unscrewing a tiny bit with each and every turn.

This went on for over three minutes, and just when that negative voice was returning in certainty and loudness and the evidence was stacking up against me ... wow. The ring passed the knuckle and slipped easily off my finger. I was so surprised I nearly dropped it!

When the jeweller finally measured my finger and the ring, she calculated that it needed to be expanded by a full two sizes. Confused, she asked, 'How on earth did you get that off your finger?'

I answered, 'I screwed it off with a mental screwdriver.'

'Oh, OK,' she replied.

WHY IT WORKS

Your mind can't tell the difference between something that happens in reality and something that you can imagine with emotional intensity. And that has a direct influence – an exact effect – on your body.

6 Make any change to your life in the fastest way possible

The fastest way to make any change in your life is to act as if that change has already been made. The name of this technique is 'As if'.

Let's go back to the memory example, where we established that whether you have a great memory or not is choice. The question is how you can switch from not remembering things to remembering them.

The fastest way to have a good memory is to act 'as if' you have a good memory. That is, you need to decide, with your entire mind, feelings and beliefs, that you have a good memory. This works for everything:

- The ego lives by: **get → do → be**. 'If I can just get something else, something more, then I will be able to do things differently, and then I will be happy and at peace. I will be me.'

- Instead, 'As If' enables us to **be → do → get**. 'I am happy and at peace. I am me, and that determines what I do, both for others and for myself, and as a result I automatically get what I wanted in the first place.'

If you become the person you really are now, then you will do (behave) in a different way, and will get results faster.

......

'THE FASTEST WAY TO MAKE ANY CHANGE IN YOUR LIFE IS TO ACT AS IF THAT CHANGE HAS ALREADY BEEN MADE.'

......

WHY IT WORKS

'As if' works because of the way we are as human beings. Three basic premises that we have already covered in the book add up to 'As if':

1. We automatically move in the direction of our most dominant thoughts.
2. What we think about, we are.
3. When we believe something to be true, we see the world that way.

Yet again, our minds cannot tell the difference between something that happens in 'reality' and something we imagine with emotional intensity. 'As if' works because it harmonizes our ego and our self immediately.

7 Make peace with your parent(s) – whether they are alive or not

This is something you have to do before you can truly be the very best that you already are and before you can be at peace while you are still alive, which is what we all ultimately seek. It may involve swallowing your pride, putting your ego to one side, and great bravery. You also must let your mother or father make peace with you. (This process also works with step-parents.)

MAKING PEACE WITH A FATHER OR MOTHER WHO IS STILL ALIVE

You may feel that your mother/father did not spend enough time with you, was too strict, or did not express love for you or pride in you. When we are young, we want to look up to our father as a role model but this might not have been possible for some reason.

You might have felt that your mother/father was too controlling – at best over-protective, at worst dominating. When we are young, we crave freedom from our mothers while still needing their unconditional love.

Whatever the outstanding issue between you, take ownership of the relationship. By taking ownership of the relationship, you reverse this. Now you take responsibility for what happened and happens in the relationship. This alone is both powerful and challenging and can bring a feeling of peace, power and certainty even before you do anything else.

The first step is to choose your moment. This moment has to be face to face and should not be made a 'big thing'. Instead, when you are alone together, talking about normal, day-to-day stuff, use a natural pause to say the following:

'Dad/Mum, while we are alone together, I want to thank you.'

He or she will reply with something like, 'What for?' Let them say whatever they choose to say, as this will now involve them in the 'discussion'. Pay attention to what they are saying with a laser focus on every word. Remember, this may be your only opportunity to do this.

When there is a silence, let the silence hang in the air for a few seconds.

You then say: 'For [the role you played in bringing me up, like when you…]' (This needs to be in your own words. The important thing is to say something general about their role in your upbringing, followed by a single specific example to illustrate it.) After you give your example, simply stop.

Your parent may react with surprise or embarrassment, or they may be receptive, or a mixture of all three. The most likely reaction will be to deny that he/she played such a big role, with some regret that they could have done more, better or something different. Again, let them speak their words, their truth and welcome them in – don't judge, just listen. This is now as much about them finding peace as it is about you.

Whatever the response, go closer to your mum or dad, look them in the eye and say, 'You brought me up in the best way that you knew how, and I want to thank you for that.'

Then pause, and if you feel it is appropriate, touch and hold their hand. Then, warmly, kindly, and with no expectation of a response, say 'I love you.'

Whatever their response, and it will most likely be positive, throw out unconditional love to him or her in your mind. Then, if you feel it is appropriate, hold each other – either cuddle or hold both their hands, while looking at them in their eyes.

And let feelings of peace, love and calm flow through you as you enjoy the reconnection with the parent who played such a big part in bringing you into, and up in, this world.

Be in the moment and totally present. You will know how it is going by how you feel it is going – you will know.

Afterwards, offer to make a cup of tea, or do something else that changes the situation.

Your parents won't live for ever, and neither will you. Please do this before it is too late. My personal experience is described in the box below.

> For years, I had complained that my father had managed my expectations when I was younger. I complained that he had rarely, if ever, told me that he loved me, and he certainly never said he was proud of me.

One day I said to my wife Rosalind that my dad had never told me that he loved me. Her reply stunned me into action. She said, 'How often have you told him that you love him?'

We arranged to visit the Lake District for a walking weekend. We met on the Friday evening and went straight for dinner. The restaurant was very full, and we chatted about family, walking and general stuff.

I then said, 'Dad, while we are together, I wanted just to say thank you.'

He replied, 'What for?'

I said, 'For taking me to my first football match.'

We both burst out laughing – our first ever football match had been a boring, dull no-score draw that had nearly put me off football for life. After discussing the match and a warm silence had settled, I said to him, 'Dad, I am so grateful for everything you have ever done for me, and the way you brought me up. I don't think I have ever told you that before.'

His response was to sit back in his seat, I think slightly nervous, surprised and embarrassed. He said something like 'Oh, no, you have nothing to thank me for' and then started looking at the menu.

My ego voice arose in my head, telling me to stop. I said 'thank you' in silence, calmly took the menu out of his hands, and then placed both my hands on his.

'I suppose what I am really trying to say, very awkwardly, is that I love you, Dad, I always have and I always will.'

No words in any dictionary or language in the world will ever describe that feeling of being connected, redemption and love. He then whispered to me, 'Those feelings are entirely reciprocated.'

I paused for a second – not exactly the words I had hoped to hear. Or were they? Of course! What he meant, what I translated his words as, and what I felt deep down, was exactly what I had said to him.

From that moment on, I was at peace with my father.

A few years later I made peace with my mother, when she was developing dementia; please don't leave it as late as I did. It is here: www.nakedleader.com/peace

......

'LET FEELINGS OF PEACE, LOVE AND CALM FLOW THROUGH YOU AS YOU ENJOY THE RECONNECTION WITH THE PARENT WHO PLAYED SUCH A BIG PART IN BRINGING YOU INTO, AND UP IN, THIS WORLD.'

......

MAKING PEACE WITH A MOTHER OR FATHER
WHO HAS DIED

Follow the same process as if they were alive, but in your mind. Imagine the whole conversation, both sides, in real time, with your parent sitting opposite you. Remember that your aim here is to be at peace with each other.

Your mind cannot tell the difference between something that happens in 'reality' and something it imagines with emotional intensity. In your mind, this will be real.

Start as you did the forgiveness session:

1. Find somewhere quiet to relax and be at peace. Cover yourself mentally with a purple cloak, or curtain. Make the colour a very deep purple; make the cloak large and sweeping, and let it flow all over you. Breathe, relax and close your eyes.

2. Now, welcome a picture and thoughts of your dad or mum to enter your mind. Acknowledge them with a warm smile as they do so, and look at his or her eyes as you do so. Your parent is some distance away from you, almost as if you are watching them on a cinema screen.

3. Your mum or dad is smiling at you with warmth, love and joy, at how wonderful it is to see you again, as if they really miss you, as if they are very grateful for this chance to say hello, to right any wrong and to just be with you.

4. Now, watch as your dad or mum steps out of the front of the cinema screen, into the cinema in which you are sitting, and slowly walk towards you.

5. They sit down next to you, look directly at you with a look of love, of absolute unconditional love, and then they take your hands in theirs.

6. And, as this happens, say to yourself, out loud or simply in your head, 'Thank you.' And then let whatever happens, happen, because it's OK. It's always OK. Always has been, always is and always will be. And then stay together for as long as you wish.

7. You are now breathing deeply, you are relaxed and totally in this moment – a moment you can let run for however long you choose.

8. When you are ready, and with a warm hug, let your mum or dad go in peace, climb back into the screen and walk away. Then they stop, they look around, and they wave. It's not a wave of goodbye but a wave of love, acknowledging the great times you had together, and that to live on in someone's heart is never to die.

9. You imagine yourself doing whatever you want to do right now. And, again, when you are ready, say to yourself with total love, 'I allow this moment to be as it is.' In this moment, and in all the moments yet to come, whoever you are, whenever you are, wherever you are.

TRUTH 8

······

YOU CAN GO DEEPER STILL

• • • • • •

I am going to ask you to look at the single word on the next page. I want you to really look, focus and give it your full attention. If any distracting thoughts enter your head as you do so, welcome them in and they will soon dissolve and disappear, allowing you to give your full awareness to the word.

As you look at the word, please imagine that the only two things that exist in entirety in those moments are you and that word. When you look at it for a few seconds, you may notice that the word becomes so important that your vision is totally focused on it, to the extent that your peripheral vision is slightly blurred.

And that's fine.

Please do this now.

STOP

Now you are back on this page, reading what you are reading, and although you have left that word behind, it could be that its meaning is still within you, taking you to a place of deeper calm, stillness and relaxation.

WORKSHOP: **Deep relaxation**

Focus your awareness on your right shoulder and notice that, as you do so, it begins to relax – feeling somehow softer, lighter and more a part of you. It is a strange feeling how focusing on one part of you makes that part become automatically more of you as a whole, and by itself feels strangely more alert and more relaxed, healthier and calmer. If you wish to extend these feelings throughout your entire body and being, all you have to do is focus your awareness, exclusively, on each part of your body, of your being, of yourself.

1. Please invest 30 seconds on each part of your body – longer if that part has been giving you issues recently (injuries, aches or pains). Again, this simple, total deeper focus may help lessen any pain you have had. And as you move your mind around your body, notice how each part you focus on causes a ripple of energy, warmth and relaxation to bloom throughout.

2. Now focus on:
  your right shoulder…
  your left shoulder…
  your right foot…
  your left foot…
  your right knee…
  your left knee.

3. Now, do the same with your fingers, one by one. Start with the little finger on either hand – a finger you may not have really given much time and attention to before. You are noticing it now, and then noticing the same on each finger in turn.

Here and now you may be aware of the quality of relaxation that you are experiencing. It's an experience that seems to take you, and calm you, deeper still.

Going into the centre of your being

......

'YOUR CENTRE ENABLES YOU TO FIND QUIET, PEACE AND CALM WITHIN YOURSELF.'

......

Next, we are going to take a mental, physical and spiritual journey to the very centre of your being.

Your centre has many names. It's known as your core in Pilates, One Point in martial arts, and in Japanese Hara or Tanden. It is physical, it is imagined, and it is the place that almost every major relaxation technique takes you to. That's what its name is out there in the world. What you choose to call it privately, deep within yourself, is entirely your choice. I will call it your centre. It is a place of peace, power and perfection, connecting your mind, body and spirit.

Your centre enables you to find quiet, peace, and calm within yourself in the midst of your busy life. It allows you to experience an ultimate sense of harmony with the universe. It is there to serve us and it does – it can and will do nothing else. It will serve you throughout your life, any and every time you choose.

All your centre does in your life is wait. It patiently waits until you trust yourself to be yourself. And now you are going there. I will be your trusted guide.

If you have been to your centre before, you may be already longing for the feelings of total peace you are about to experience once again.

If you have never been there before, you may be tingling with anticipation at the thought of finding your very own peaceful private and personal place for the first time.

......
`ALL YOUR CENTRE DOES IN YOUR LIFE IS
WAIT. IT PATIENTLY WAITS UNTIL YOU
TRUST YOURSELF TO BE YOURSELF.'
......

WORKSHOP:
Going to your centre

1. Place one of your index fingers on your belly button
and hold it there. Then place your other hand flat on
your stomach below your finger – the upper edge
of the flat hand should be touching the underside of
your index finger.

2. Now remove your finger from your belly button, and
use it to find the centre of the hand that is flat on
your stomach. Imagine a place in line with the point
of your finger. It sits further back inside your body,
inside the very centre of you. This is why we call
this – the centre of your mind, body and spirit – your
centre.

3. Before we go there, first take a deep breath and, as
you exhale, relax completely.

4. Say 'Thank you' to your ego voice and allow it to go quiet. If it takes a little longer to go quiet, that's OK.

5. Remember, allow yourself to think any and every thought you have. In fact, welcome them in, love each thought as it comes in. And they will simply dissolve and disappear.

When you notice your breathing, you'll realize that your self has been breathing for you all along. And the thought, the knowledge, the idea of this may help you relax even more.

Now focus your attention on the word on the next page, and, as you read the word and take in its meaning, count silently in your head from 10 down to 1, and then to zero. Whenever you combine a visual word such as this with a mental activity of counting down, your Spiritual Everlasting Loving Friend will take over, with your Earth Guiding Officer's total permission.

STILL

Soon, silence will have passed into legend. Now it has passed into your life.

Amid a world of phones, chatter and endless noise – silence. OK, thank you.

Workshop:
The path to peace

Now for the adventure, the path to peace, purely at an ego level before we find total peace in Truth 9.

1. Place one hand flat on your centre, as you did earlier. Notice any warm, calming and centred feelings you have.

2. Take a deep breath and, as you exhale, relax completely.

3. Now bring to mind a challenging person or situation. When you have done so, place a finger from your free hand in the middle of your forehead. This signifies the location of the thought.

4. Think for a moment how that issue, problem or challenge is making you feel. It probably makes you feel or act in a way that is unhelpful to resolving it.

5. Begin slowly moving your finger down, and, as it does, imagine the unhelpful feeling is literally travelling down with it.

6. As you 'travel', with all of your mind, body and spirit, your feelings are about to be transformed.

7. With your mind, follow your finger all the way down, until it reaches your other hand that is still flat on your centre.

8. As soon as your finger touches this hand that is protecting your centre, you should begin to have feeling of such warmth, calmness and positive energy that it transcends words. It is a wondrous feeling that deepens in glorious strength every time you breathe.

And why wouldn't it be so amazing? After all, it is you, the centre of you, your centre as it always has been, always will be and as it is right now. As you read, those miraculous sensations of relaxation, confidence and being centred are perhaps doubling now. And now they are doubling again.

And now you are returning to you, your self, the self that you once were, the self you always will be. And the self you are right now. And now you have arrived back to where you always have been, you may feel a rush of familiarity pass through you. And why wouldn't you? This is a familiar place. You have remembered where you always were, you have returned and, above all, you have arrived at the natural, perfect, place of peace, of being – of you.

And now it is time to bring everything together.

The next Truth – Truth 9 – completes this book. It completes your journey home, back to where you once were, where you have always been and perhaps not realized – back to you. It brings together all the Truths by combining all I have written, all you have read and everything that has happened in our lives – mine and yours – to a single point.

Truth 9 will finally bring you back to where you have always yearned to be: it will bring you back to you. It will return you to yourself.

It is powerful, and the results are amazing. Are you ready…?

TRUTH 9

......

IT'S DOWN TO YOU

• • • • • •

Here are the Truths of this book so far:

- **Truth 1:** Your success never happens by chance; it always happens by choice.

- **Truth 2:** There is nothing 'wrong' with you.

- **Truth 3:** You get unconditional love by giving it.

- **Truth 4:** Your life means whatever you choose it to mean.

- **Truth 5:** Your ego voice quietens with 'Thank you'.

- **Truth 6:** You do what you do based on choices and your self-esteem, to move towards pleasure or away from pain.

- **Truth 7:** Your imaginary fears need imaginary solutions and your real challenges need real solutions.

- **Truth 8:** Your journey to the centre of you goes deeper still.

Everything I have written and all you have read have brought you to this moment, and there are two conclusions:

1. It is simply not possible for you to experience something you did not naturally know on the day you were born, as long as you welcome, embrace and allow that feeling in, with total expectation, warmth and love.

2. It is simply certain that you will experience something you did naturally know on the day you were born, as long as you welcome, embrace and allow that feeling in, with total expectation, warmth and love.

End of. No, to be more accurate … return of. The return of you to being you.

Now, how on earth, or on any other planet you may choose to visit, can all the Truths in this book be brought together as one, so that at last you will discover who you really are – so that at last you 'find' yourself.

The answer has to be simple. It has to be memorable, and it has to be so powerful, practical and proven that it will 'work' for you, straight away.

And the answer lies in just nine short words. Just nine magic words will:

- move you from war to peace
- from conflict, both inner and outer, to absolute calm
- from living either in the past or the future to being in the present.

And here they are on the next page. They deserve a page of their own.

Please read them and reread them again and again, several times. S l o w l y.

And as you read, as you focus your awareness on the words, the spaces in between and even on the important little comma, you will take in every letter, every word, and every pause in between. And as you do, you may notice a deep sense of peace flooding through you. This may happen straight away or it may take a little longer. Because what you focus on becomes real. It may take one reading, or more, to experience a sense of relaxation, stillness and calm settling over and within yourself. You might find yourself thinking about how these nine words can be bringing you whatever feelings they are bringing; you could find yourself with a clearer mind; perhaps you are feeling almost empty. Or maybe you have simply found your self.

......

`THE ANSWER LIES IN JUST NINE SHORT WORDS...´

......

`WHEN YOU LOVE WHAT IS,
THE WAR IS OVER.´

When you love what is, the war is over

And that's it. Or, to be more precise, that's them. Or, to be even more precise, that's you.

Remember, this isn't a 'fix' – you can't be fixed because there was never anything 'wrong' with you. And that's not you 'done' – you are not a roast dinner, either. You are, though, back where you started.

Your being born was a miracle, and you are still a miracle today. On that miraculous day, you had everything you needed to achieve literally anything you wanted, just as you still have today.

Right now.

It took you nine months to be born. It will take nine words to bring you home to a place of calm and wellbeing that you may not have experienced for years – so long ago you may not even remember it. In a world full of so-called 'self-help' and 'Mind, Body and Spirit' books, could it be possible, could it just be possible, that all of the angst these so many books are addressing can be removed with just nine words?

······

'YOUR BEING BORN WAS A MIRACLE, AND YOU ARE STILL A MIRACLE TODAY.'

······

Billions of words in millions of books from thousands of authors, brought together in one single sentence:

••••••

'WHEN YOU LOVE WHAT IS, THE WAR IS OVER.'

••••••

As you read these words again, at a speed that is comfortable for you, it may be that you are taking slower breaths and your heartbeat is slowing. These things are happening easily, effortlessly and automatically. Because the moment you let go of your battles and open your heart to the power of what is, you come to rest, at peace and at one with the present moment. The now. This is the beginning and the end of your self-help, emotional and spiritual journey. It all begins, and ends where it begins, with you, just as you are.

WHY ARE THESE WORDS SO POWERFUL?

We have already established that there is no 'right' or 'wrong'. There is only what works and what doesn't, what helps you and what hurts you. In other words, what works is what takes you and people you know closer to what you want to achieve, and what doesn't takes you further away.

Over the last 20 years, I have been obsessed with what works and what always works, with every human being, from every country and culture with whatever beliefs, every time – with minimal effort, maximum speed and lasting effects. And having observed, discovered and applied the techniques, I have carried out the ultimate scientific test by asking, 'Does it work every time, for a large number of people?' It's not about whether it works in theory, or in academia, but in real life.

Yes or no?

If it works, it works.

And it does.

The overall premise of this book is that you are you, and that is all you ever need to be. It has equipped you with the tools and techniques to help you achieve this, all of which have been researched by many kinds of people, from children (who really 'get' this stuff) all the way to the most highly regarded academics.

If something, anything, 'works' for you in any area of your life, then you should do it, and keep doing it, just as long as you are not hurting or harming anyone. And when you are truly yourself, you will have no wish ever to hurt anyone, ever.

It's total common sense, in a world where sense isn't actually that common.

Until now, that is.

Remember, if it works, it works.

If it doesn't work, then do something else and keep taking different actions until something does work.

Academics may call this 'simplistic' but that doesn't matter – all that matters is whether it works for you or not. And it does. It has to. Because, with all due respect to you and the rest of humanity, we adore, need and crave simplicity.

How can you apply these words to any event, experience and eventuality in your life? When I explain how to apply them, everything will come together to answer the biggest question of them all:

Who are you, really?

······

`YOU ARE YOU, AND THAT IS ALL YOU EVER NEED TO BE.´

······

WORKSHOP: How to remove any thought, feeling or emotion you don't want

This is a simple exercise that is similar to how you quietened your ego voice in Truth 5, and deeper... Whenever you have a thought, feeling or emotion that you do not want to have, you need to allow it, welcome it, and give it total and unconditional permission to enter your head. And you do this as follows:

1. Right now think of an experience you have had in the past that made you feel upset, worried, scared, or angry, or made you have any other feeling that

you did not want. Think of a time, a place, an event where you had a feeling that you did not want. See what you saw, hear what you heard and feel what you felt.

2. Take a few moments to do this.

3. Now you have recreated that feeling, rate its strength on a scale of 0 to 10, 10 being the strongest and most unpleasant feeling you've ever had, 0 being perfect bliss, Zen-like calm.

4. Give your feeling a general name, such as 'worry'. However, if that word doesn't work for you, simply substitute your own negative word(s) each time you see the word 'worry', such as 'stress' or 'be angry'.

5. Now say to yourself, in silence, with love and calmness, and letting whatever happens, happen: 'I allow myself to worry.'

6. Now rate the strength of the feeling you had, on a scale of 0 to 10, 10 being the strongest and most unpleasant feeling you've ever had, 0 being perfect bliss, Zen-like calm.

7. How weird, strange and bizarre is that?

8. Before we talk about what just happened ... go and sit in a place where you can relax and give yourself

total permission to give yourself over to whatever happens next – everything will be OK.

9. Again, please say to yourself, in silence, with love and calmness, and letting whatever happens, happen: 'I allow myself to worry.'

10. And this time now say, 'Worry – bring it on! I want to worry more! Call that worry? Come on – I want more, more more!'

And now you couldn't worry if your life depended on it.

WHAT JUST HAPPENED?

As you will know by now, you were born with only two fears: falling over and loud noises. That means you had only two 'natural' fears that were an innate part of you. Although you probably got over those fears, let us go back to the day of your birth where there were just those two fears.

When you have a feeling you do not want, like worry, and you want it gone, the usual tactic most of us adopt is to fight it. However, as we now know from Truth 5, that doesn't work. In fact, it has the reverse effect: it actually makes the feeling you want to get rid of more powerful and increase its stranglehold over you.

The irony of ironies is that the very strategy we most often adopt to try to remove our fears, worries and negative emotions is the very reason they exist in the first place. Remember: it is simply not possible for you to experience something you did not naturally know on the day you were born, as long as you welcome, embrace and allow that feeling in, with total expectation, warmth and love.

And so, when you welcome in, with total permission, desire and love, any feeling you did not have on the day you were born, that feeling will have nowhere to go, and so it will enter, dissolve and disappear. More specifically, just as in the previous Truth, the feeling will enter your head, it will run down through your neck, past your chest, and into the very centre of your being – your centre – where it will complete itself, dissolve and disappear.

It can do nothing else, as it is not a natural part of you. Your centre makes an immediate assessment of this feeling and asks itself, 'Is this a natural feeling, a part of me that I had on the day I was born?'

It then answers itself – in the case of unhelpful feelings – 'no'. And so, with nowhere to go, it leaves you, and you can actually feel it leaving you. In fact, it completes itself, dissolves and disappears.

From this very moment – right now – you are perhaps choosing to be no longer trapped by any negative thoughts, feelings or opinions in the way that you were used to before. Because when you open that door in your mind and welcome those thoughts in – and love them coming in, they have nowhere to go. And so they complete themselves, dissolve and simply, gently, magically disappear – like letters drawn on water with a finger.

WORKSHOP:
How to grow, heighten and increase a thought, feeling or emotion that you do want

Whenever you have a thought, a feeling or an emotion that you do want, allow it, welcome it, and give it total and unconditional permission to enter your head. Then do the following:

1. Right now, think of an experience you have had in the past that made you feel ecstatic, calm, confident, inspired, or made you have any other feeling that you really wanted. Think of a time, a place or an event where you had such a feeling – one you really wanted – and see what you saw, hear what you heard and feel what you felt.

2. Take a few moments to do this.

3. Now you have recreated that feeling, rate its strength on a scale of 0 to 10, 10 being the strongest or most pleasant, 0 being a place of fear.

4. Give your feeling a general name, such as 'happy'. However, if that word doesn't work for you, simply substitute your own positive word each time you see 'happy'.

5. Now say to yourself, in silence, with love and calmness, and letting whatever happens, happen: 'I allow myself to be happy.'

6. Now rate the strength of the positive feeling again, having said those words, on a scale of 0 to 10 – 10 being the strongest and most pleasant, 0 being a place of fear.

7. Again, please say to yourself, in silence, with love and calmness, and letting whatever happens, happen: 'I allow myself to be happy.'

And this time now say, 'I allow myself to be here, in this present moment.' This is the bravest, boldest most beautiful permission you can ever give yourself – to dare, dream and deserve to be your self: 'I allow myself to be me.' Please don't keep your self to yourself.

WHAT JUST HAPPENED?

On the day you were born you were full of joy, fun, delight, bliss, ecstasy, confidence, trust, belief, faith and happiness. You were happy, and you can be again. You can feel any of those feelings that you had on the day you were born, if you only welcome them in.

Remember, it is simply certain that you will experience something you did naturally know on the day that you were born, as long as you welcome, embrace and allow that feeling in, with total expectation, warmth and love.

This time, the feeling started in your centre and spread with a glow and flow of warmth. Like warm and wonderful water in a lovely piping-hot bath, it will flow all around your body, reaching every part of your mind, body and spirit. And as it flows, it will become stonger.

......

'YOU CAN FEEL ANY OF THE FEELINGS YOU
HAD ON THE DAY YOU WERE
BORN, IF YOU WELCOME THEM IN.'

......

The Golden Rule of Peace

Welcome in, with total permission, every desire and every feeling you have. Every thought, idea and emotion – bring it in.

If it was a feeling you did not have on the day you were born, a feeling that is unhelpful and does not serve you, it will travel into your head, down through your body and arrive at your centre, where it will complete itself, dissolve and disappear.

If it was a feeling you did have on the day you were born, a feeling that is helpful and serves you, it will start in your centre and travel all around your body, warming, healing, inspiring every part of your being. And it will stay with you, for as long as you choose.

In short – if it is a natural part of you it will grow; if not, it will go.

Happiness is wanting what you get

Success is getting what you want.

Happiness is wanting what you get.

There it is, like so many of the answers in life, right before our very eyes, and hidden in plain sight.

Happiness, peace, your answer – maybe even *the* answer – is wanting what you get.

Allowing each moment to be as it is puts you in a powerful position to decide how you react and respond to it, and empowers you then to change something if you want.

WORKSHOP:
The biggest question of all

1. Visit a quiet, relaxing spot that is one of your favourite places to be – not in your mind, in reality.

2. Sit, relax, and be still.

3. Quieten your inner voice with 'Thank you.'

4. Know that what you are about to do is OK. Then, softly, slowly and with huge expectations, close your eyes and ask yourself: 'Who am I and why am I here?'

5. And then open your eyes.

6. And then forget the question. For it is in the moment when you stop asking that the answer will arrive.

7. Expect it to arrive.

And look out for life showing you the way. It will. All around you, things will happen that will help you: people and events will take on a new significance; synchronicities will happen all around you, both with you and to you.

......
'WHO ARE YOU AND WHY ARE YOU HERE?'
......

A synchronicity is a 'meaningful coincidence' – like when you are about to call someone and they call you. The thing about synchronicity is you have to believe in it for it to happen. The other thing about synchronicity – and why it's so different from coincidence – is this: you have to actually do something – to act – as a result of the synchronicity.

The greatest mystery of life is who you truly are.

And now, life will show and share with you that answer. Be on the lookout: it will come from somewhere, perhaps when you least expect it.

And then do something about it.

You can experience the answers to your biggest questions as if you already know them, by giving total and absolute attention to everyone and everything that happens around you. Life will always show you the way, much like the way you are experiencing these words as if they are little bubbles of relaxation, floating into your mind, soothing your thoughts.

You will find the answer to the biggest question because life knows who you are and why you are here. It knows the reason you were born and the life you were born to live. It is a life that cannot be 'won' or 'lost' – only lived, and lived by you.

We each get one life, one go, one turn. And when life shows you, you will know who you are, why you are here, and you will be.

Simply be. And as you are, it is as if you are travelling in your mind, right now, on your path, your journey, your adventure back to where you have come from, back to where you have always been. It's a wonderful, wondrous and warm place that you can now remember, rekindle and return to.

It's a place where you can be the true you.

Here and now.

Right now.

......

'WE EACH GET ONE LIFE, ONE GO, ONE TURN.'

......

Imagine if you simply could not fail

What would you do?
Where would you go?
Who would you be?

Imagine if you simply could not fail:

- What would you do? You would do anything.
- Where would you go? You would go anywhere.
- Who would you be? You would decide, very simply, to be *you*.

Because that is all you ever need to be. What you seek, you already are, all you were on the day you were born and all you are today, and all you will be every day going forward.

·······

YOU MAY AT TIMES HAVE FELT
A LITTLE LOST IN LIFE.

NO MORE.

YOU ARE HERE, RIGHT NOW.

YOU ARE FOUND.

WELCOME HOME.

·······

THANK YOU...

To my family:

Rosalind for support, love, oh yes, and comments.

Anthony for initial proofreading and Olivia for general counsel, and the skating.

To Tina Barnard, Sally Hodgkins and Judith Sergeant for comments.

To Lou Rose for the Pilates and guidance on Hara, core and the centre.

To Professor Colin Turner – it was in Colin's book *Shooting the Monkey* that I first discovered the terms 'Spiritual Everlasting Loving Friend' and 'Earth Guiding Officer'. He now feels they have gone into the natural language; however, I wanted to thank you, Colin.

If I have used any phrase, quote or anything else that you believe belongs to you, then please let me know and it will be corrected in a future edition.

Huge thanks to Iain Campbell and Jonathan Shipley at John Murray Learning.

And, most of all, thanks to you for reading this far... even if you haven't.

David X